Scarr's Pizza

4c

4 COLOR BOOKS
An imprint of TEN SPEED PRESS
California | New York

SCARR PIMENTEL

with Kimberly Chou Tsun An

PHOTOGRAPHY BY KOKI SATO

THE SCARR'S PIZZA COOKBOOK

NEW YORK–STYLE PIZZA FOR EVERYBODY

THE MOON

ll Step for Man, a Leap for Mankind

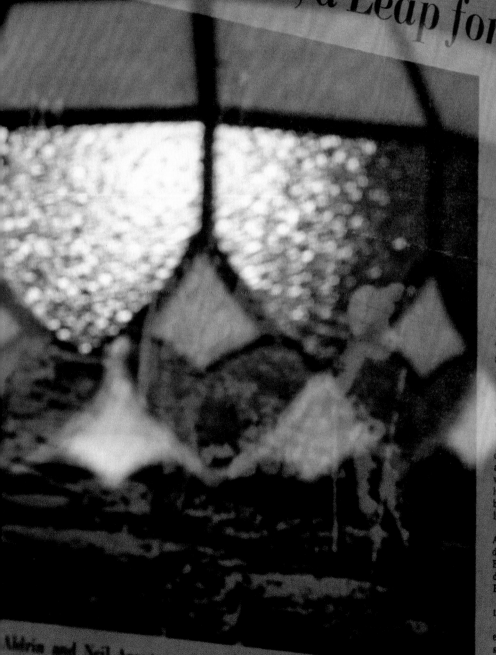

Aldrin and Neil Armstrong Plant the U.S. Flag on the Lunar Surface

It's 'Magnificent Desolation'

Landscape's Like Southwest U.S., Armstrong Says

By ROBERT S. BOYD
Chief Of The Washington Bureau

HOUSTON — Man landed and w
on the moon Sunday.

The fragile spaceship Eagle depe
American astronauts Neil Armstrong
Edwin (Buzz) Aldrin in the barren S
west corner of the Sea of Tranquil
4:18 p.m., and six and a half hours
at 20 seconds past 10:56 p.m., Arms
planted his left foot on the moon.

"That's one small step for man
lant leap for mankind . . ." were his
words.

In his normally calm voice tremulous w
citement, the first man on the moon radioed a
account of history's greatest adventure back t
while a TV camera beamed live pictures of the
lunar landscape to a spell-
bound audience of mil-
lions.

Twenty minutes later,
Armstrong talked Aldrin
down the ladder of the
Eagle onto the firm, pow-
dery soil of Tranquility
Base.

"Magnificent desola-
tion," Aldrin called it.

Thus was completed an
epic journey charted eight years ago but drea
since man first lifted his eyes toward the heave

For a few brief hours Sunday night, the
life on the moon. Two-legged creatures from th
et Earth talked, walked, ran and worked on t
of an alien world.

4 Pages Inside

Moon's Triumph
World Elated
Wives Proud
No Soft Shoe
The Descent

CONTENTS

PIZZA

EXTRAS

THE NEIGHBORHOOD

BEST IN THE CITY

BY DJ CLARK KENT

Scarr's . . . one of my favorite New York City stories.

Scarr Pimentel is the epitome of a NYC guy. He lives at the corner of Real and Honorable. They don't make them like us anymore. We are both from the hood—Hispanic and honest. But let's stick to him. He comes from the bottoms. He ran the tough NYC streets. He learned how to survive on the job. He knew he didn't want to end up the wrong way. He has seen everything that NYC streets can show you. Maybe too much. But, it made him the *best*. Along the way, he found food as a way to express himself. He worked in a few spots to get it right. And, man, did he get it *right*.

The first time I tried Scarr's Pizza, I knew I had a new favorite. Our mutual friend Audie made me try it. Now, I'm a serious pizza guy, so this was a big test. I was attending an art show up the block from the shop, which made it easy to check the place out. The shop screamed old, around-the-way pizza joint: dimly lit, wood-paneled walls, old-school signs, vintage seats and tables, small bar with fixed stools—*super* NYC.

Then the pizza—perfect. No, seriously, it's perfect. The texture, crust, sauce, cheese, beef pepperoni or chicken sausage. . . all exceptionally balanced. Oh, did I mention they have vegan pizza? Yeah. . . that too. Let's not forget the salad—incredible. Last, the DJ CK Lemonade. Thank me later. But, back to the guy. We quickly became friends. Maybe because it seems like he is a younger reflection of myself. Scarr the person is a stellar individual. He cares about everything, about everybody. He is that glimmer of magic that only NYC streets can create. We are brothers of the same mind. We both love fly shit! This made it simple to want to do cool things with him. That's how the idea of me making a shoe to celebrate our friendship and his success happened.

I wanted to make something that spoke to both of us. Great classic NYC street gear and good sneakers with the New York City flag and sports team colors, Scarr's branding, elevated materials, and personal messaging. Only for his friends and family—perfect because they mean so much to him.

Scarr's is the best pizza and pizza shop in NYC. But Scarr is one of the best people on the planet. (Meagan too!)

I love you, both.

DJ Clark Kent

INTRO

A NEW YORK THING

Pizza is synonymous with New York. I don't view it as an Italian thing. Especially slice pizza. It was born here, you know what I'm saying?

It caters to everyone. It's not a bougie thing; it's super accessible and anyone can have it. It's what I always wanted in opening a spot, specifically a shop like what I grew up with in the city, where anybody could line up for an affordable slice and everybody got treated the same.

I fell in love with pizza because it brings people together from all over. It forces them to congregate and talk to each other. Slice-shop culture with counter service is different from being in a sit-down restaurant. In my shop, you get someone from Middle America next to someone who grew up in the hood here. You'll see a Muslim person next to a Jewish person waiting on line together. We get photographers, construction workers, building supers, regular people from the neighborhood. You don't see that anywhere else. It's democratic. That's what makes New York slice pizza beautiful.

When I talk about New York–style pizza, I mean pizza how the old-school spots where I learned to make pizza used to do it. And the way I do it is a big slice, thin but sturdy enough to fold, crispy but soft, with the perfect balance of crust, sauce, and cheese. No one truly does New York–style pizza like how I do it, using fresh-milled organic flour and all-natural ingredients. There's nothing like it.

For me, pizza was the one thing that always made sense. When we were kids, it was what we could afford if we had a couple dollars in our pockets. When we were hungry, it was the go-to and a quick meal. The shop was our meeting place. There was no dollar menu when I was a kid, but pizza was always there.

And there wasn't ever an option that was healthy with organic or all-natural ingredients. On top of that, I felt like the quality of slice pizza went down from what it used to be. From working in pizza shops and being in the restaurant industry over the years, I saw where people started cutting costs once they were able to access cheaper, subpar ingredients when low-cost wholesale distributors came on the scene.

So after years of working at these spots, learning the ropes, and then running other people's shops—as well as lots of research in my free time—I was like, you know what? Let me make a New York–style pizza that tastes great and uses good ingredients and fresh-milled wheat but doesn't taste like it's whole grain. It has that New York flavor profile and texture *and* it's healthier—that was the goal for me. That's what I created, and still, no one else today does it.

I know we're the best pizza in the city, and in the world, in my opinion. People love us. And I'm talking mad people, including outside of just the pizza or food worlds. It's everybody from car people to fashion people who follow us, support, and come through. I like that. But our community actually loves everything about the shop, not just the pizza, the staff, or the space. They love the brand; they love the story. It's a real story. I just do me. I do New York shit. That's all I know, and people see that. That's the beauty and what I love.

UPTOWN

I grew up Uptown for most of my life and was raised in a large extended family. Both of my parents came here from the Dominican Republic in the 1970s. My mom came over to New York when she was a teenager, and then met my dad when they were set up by one of her sisters who was working in a textile factory with my dad's cousin at the time. Besides my parents and brothers, I was surrounded by cousins, aunts, uncles, my grandma—everyone trying to take care of us and make a living. All of that shaped me. Even if I didn't know it at the time, it put me on the path I'm on now.

I did always know I wanted to open up a restaurant and be in food. But I didn't know what at first specifically. I originally thought it was going to be a Dominican restaurant, maybe Spanish food, because my mom was a good cook and that's what she was known for.

My mom is one of five siblings. She has three sisters and a brother. Everyone says, "Oh, my mom cooks great." But I really knew *my* mom was a great cook when all her sisters would tell her to make food for family get-togethers. Cousins were always asking if she was cooking or my friends were coming over to the house to eat, stuff like that. That's part of what got me started.

My family was always cooking, and it was always Spanish food. My favorite dish was what we called kipe or quipe. Our version was barley mixed with ground lamb or ground beef, which we'd eat with hot sauce. It actually comes from the Lebanese influence in the DR; it's called kibbeh in Arabic. My mom also makes pilaf-style rice, a really good flan, and I love her fried plantains too.

Both of my parents worked with food in different ways, sometimes together. When we were kids, my dad got started with a boxed-lunch truck in the Bronx, and my mom

would make sandwiches for the truck. Then he owned a diner for a few years where my mom would help out too.

But really, it all came from my grandmother. Not just my love for food, but also for the people and the atmosphere that make up a restaurant experience. When I talk about my grandmother Tita, she's actually my mom's oldest sister. She basically helped raise my mom, then me and my brothers.

Tita had her own café back in the DR. She was the first of our family, on my mom's side, to come over in the late 1960s. Slowly, she started getting other family members over with visas and then green cards.

As kids, me and my brothers would stay at Tita's house every weekend. She needed my mom's help with things and would babysit us in exchange. Tita worked in a diner on the Upper West Side, at 77th and Columbus, for a long time. A Black Cuban lady named Elena owned it, and they served really good Cuban food. Everyone in the neighborhood knew Elena and Tita.

I loved the environment of it. Every time you went in there, you met someone new. People who lived and worked in the neighborhood were regulars, and the regulars became your family. It was just about the food and the people, and it really felt like an extension of Elena's and Tita's living rooms.

Most places were like that back in the day. They knew you and they remembered your name. People at Elena's used to help me with my homework after school. I always sat at the counter, and I'd get rice and beans or stewed chicken. I can think of only a few places in the city that are still like that now.

Growing up wasn't easy, but restaurants were a way for us. My parents didn't have the same opportunities as other people to build generational wealth because of coming here from the DR, not speaking English as a first language, and so on.

If you didn't want to work in a corporate office and you were an immigrant, or Black, or both, it was just easier to work in a restaurant and have a chance of moving up. Even going to school, and hoping it would one day pay off, wasn't a guarantee. Quick money in their time was either on the streets or in the food industry. So that's what we did.

I got my first taste of it working at Emilio's Ballato when I was seventeen.

DOWNTOWN

I didn't know about Ballato's at the time. Now it's famous. It's a downtown institution in Nolita with really good old-school Italian food. Lots of celebrities hang out there. I started working there maybe a year or two after the owner, Emilio Vitolo Sr., bought it in the 1990s from the Ballato family.

My friend's mom used to be the general manager at Lombardi's—it was the first pizzeria in the United States—and she was friends with Emilio Sr. She was Italian American, and so was everyone else who worked at Lombardi's, so they weren't going to hire me there. She wasn't involved in any street stuff, but she knew how I was. I was a little wild at the time. Normal New York shit. She was like, "I need him off the street!"

So even though I wasn't an Italian, she told Emilio, "Hire this kid. You need a busser; you need people." Emilio was up to here with bills, but she convinced him to give me a job as a busboy. Then I moved up to server. We were in the middle of Downtown, right on Houston Street, near SoHo. The restaurant had a back room where famous people, or people Emilio knew, could go for a little more privacy. I saw the Evander Holyfield and Mike Tyson fight working in the back room. His friends there that night wanted me to serve them. We had a blast. I have a ton of stories from that time.

But then after a couple years, I wanted to try something different. I started selling cellphones and beepers on 125th Street. It was 1999 and I was nineteen. It was the golden era of hip-hop, before Harlem got somewhat gentrified, and I met all the rappers there. I sold beepers to Jim Jones before he became popular, I met Cam'ron, and I saw Jay-Z and Dame Dash.

I got into trouble out here and went down to Miami for a little bit,

around the time my parents had moved there.

When I came back to New York, I ended up working at Lombardi's again. I started off by taking phone orders to get used to the fast pace. We had three phones ringing off the hook at prime time, and we would take orders and write them down.

It was different back then, Lombardi's as well as the neighborhood. This was before Nolita blew up. There were lots of independent businesses, and people said hello to each other and seemed to look out for one another. There were also more locals around and fewer tourists. I was still a young kid meeting all these cool people. Some of the people I met down there I still see around. Then, one of the servers quit, so I switched to doing that, and I started making good money. Being in restaurants was working for me.

And then I started learning to make pizza.

There was a Puerto Rican dude named Ariel who made the pizza at Lombardi's. He got the job after coming out of jail because he was dating my friend's mom's friend. He was always cool with us, but he was very, very New York, let me put it that way. And I'll always appreciate that he noticed I was interested and took the time to show me what he was doing. I started watching, and he started teaching me little by little how to make pizza—how to open the dough, cook it, stuff like that. I wasn't no maestro at the time, but I'm a quick learner. I've always

been. Working there, watching the pizza guys, you get the general idea of how to make it.

I stayed for four or five years. But then my friend's mom, who was still the GM, passed. After that, ownership changed, and we didn't get along. I had to move on. From there I went and worked at other pizza spots: first L'asso, then Artichoke, then Joe's, and a few places I don't need to name. I've worked all over, and I've consulted. I even took a break and worked in TV production, but that burned me out. I always came back to food though. And I always came back to pizza.

From all this, I learned not only how to make really good pizza but also how I wanted to do things—healthier and with better ingredients.

I also learned how I wanted to run a business. I saw how other people ran their shops without respect for their staff or their product. I've been in positions where I worked 100 hours a week, ran the spaces like they were my own, took care of everyone, and raised their profit margins. But the people who had all the power favored their friends, changed their minds, or otherwise stole opportunities from me. I knew when I had the chance, I would do it differently.

I don't consider it shit-talking if I'm being honest, you know?

THE DR

I went to visit my grandmother, my mom's mom, in the DR as a kid with my parents and brothers. She lived in the country and had land with chickens on it.

One of the days we were visiting, we had chicken for dinner. My brother saw it and was like, "Don't eat it! They grabbed the chicken we were playing with, broke its neck, and plucked it!"

We were playing with that chicken like an hour prior before they killed it. And I was like, "Oh man, they don't go to the supermarket?" I didn't realize they didn't have any in the countryside. Back in the city, we were used to seeing chicken at the butcher shop, or already chopped up and frozen in packs at the grocery store.

But I ate it and it was amazing. It was the best chicken I ever had in my life. Also the best rice and beans. The best everything actually. That was my first experience of seeing where something really came from and realizing how different it could be. I was seven or eight years old.

I'm lucky to have eaten all over the world. But that chicken is still one of the best things I've ever had.

We only went back to the DR two or three times as a family when I was a kid. With three kids and both parents working we couldn't afford to go there often. But Tita had a little extra money through her side hustles.

My mother's family grew up in the countryside. My dad's family came from the city.

I knew what poverty was like here, being in the hood. When I was growing up, there were crack vials everywhere, and you had to watch out for needles in the street. But most people really don't understand what poverty is until they go to the city in a developing country, like the DR, and see it for themselves. Even I didn't get it at the time. The kids I met out there were running barefoot in the hot sun on asphalt. People would show up and ask me for all my things, and I was like, "Bro, I'm poor too!" I had brought my own cereal with me, and all the other kids wanted to try it. They'd never had Cap'n Crunch before.

My father saw how I was treating the kids in the neighborhood where he grew up. So he tells me, "These guys are poorer than us. Share your stuff with everybody. When you leave, promise me you're going to give away all your stuff. Just wear the clothes on your back. Give away your sneakers, give away everything."

And I did. At first, I didn't want to. I was a little kid and I liked my stuff. But then I understood. I gave away everything, even this little Mickey Mouse watch that I really liked.

That's when I learned not to be so selfish. Even though you think you have nothing, there are people out there who have even less than you. People who can't properly clothe or feed themselves, and it's not their fault.

To this day, I always want to help kids in the neighborhood and put them on if I can. You should always make sure your people are good.

30

SCARR'S PIZZA

In 2016, it was time for me to do my own thing. I didn't want to work for anyone else but myself. My boy showed up, threw fifty bands on the table, and said, "I wanna invest. Let's do it." I was saving up money with my wife, Meagan, who is also my business partner. I knew we didn't have enough yet, but I was like, "Fuck it, the money will come."

Then my other friend invested in it, and that was it. We opened up in the red, our first space at 22 Orchard Street between Canal and Hester, on the border of the Lower East Side and Chinatown, 750 square feet, with a counter in the front and a small bar and four booths in the back. We milled our own flour and did all the prep in the basement. This was before that part of the neighborhood became what it is now. New shops and cafés were starting to open up, but also hole-in-the-wall restaurants and mom-and-pop businesses were still holding on.

It was a little scary the first three months, to be honest with you. I had to borrow money. But I knew what I had to do, which was work the shop myself, and I didn't mind. It was me, my friend Los, my partners, and eventually a couple of prep guys. All day, every day. Meagan would even come to the shop after her day job and help behind the bar. Slowly, I found people and trained them to make pizza.

Ever since I was young, I've been coming Downtown. As a teenager, I liked to come down and go to stores such as Canal Jeans, Yellow Rat Bastard, Michael K, the flea market on Broadway, Tower Records, and Coconut Records. The neighborhood has changed a lot. Most of these places aren't around anymore. Independent places have turned into chains, or the buildings they were in got torn down for new development. I used to hang out at Jerry's, a diner on Prince Street, which eventually got taken over by some boutique. I had friends Uptown and friends Downtown. But I've always been drawn to the energy in New York below 14th Street. Downtown Manhattan has always been the mecca of fashion, music, and everything for decades. The coolest, most creative people made it

what it was. There was always something happening. That part of New York is slowly going away.

I didn't always know how, or when, but I knew that when I opened up my own spot it would be down here. No matter what, I had to do it here, even if the rent was higher than everywhere else. Because I was born and raised here and worked my ass off to get to where I am. I am a true New York story. I grew up with no money, and I opened the shop with no money.

I always knew I wanted Scarr's to be Downtown, but not somewhere super gentrified or overrun with tourists. I wanted it to be a chill spot. That's why I built it in a small space, and that's all I could afford at the time. And it *was* chill for the first couple of years.

I wanted something that represented us and growing up here, and pizzerias from the past—from the quality of the food to the vibe to the music to the look.

In terms of the aesthetic, it was an homage to the spots we used to go to as kids in New York but more modern. The wood paneling is the same stuff they use in mid-century modern homes in Palm Springs. It's actually from the 1960s, and it's real wood that you have to special order.

The brand colors blue, white, and orange were inspired by the New York City flag which I used to stare at when I was in the auditorium in elementary school. That always resonated with me. No one had ever used the flag colors and design the way we did. We came out with it first, and then some designer stole that idea from us. We've been copied a lot since we started. (Listen, it's fine with me if you're from New York, use the colors.) I'm not going to name the spots, but there are people who opened up after me, threw money at an idea, and tried to imitate us. But it's never the same. It's not genuine

and there's no heart or swag behind it. There's something different about really growing up here and finding your way despite all the odds stacked against us—and then creating something that is really for everyone but speaks to other New Yorkers who grew up like me.

Now, Scarr's Pizza is successful. After the first couple of years mostly serving locals and growing through word of mouth, we blew up. We have lines going down the block for slices. People come from all over the city and all over the world.

Over time, we've gotten more attention from food media and food people. But they all do that on their own accord. We don't sell out and we don't pay for PR. I know how conversations around food have changed so much with social media, trends, and all of that. But I'm not interested in any of it. I treat everyone the same way I want to be treated. I welcome whoever finds their way to the shop. I know that my pizza is the best, period. And even in the early days, even when we weren't as popular, I knew that over time, no matter what, if I made the best product, people would come. It's as genuine as you can get.

Since then we've opened up more spots. But we're still doing it our way, with stone-milled flour local to each region and a focus on good ingredients, keeping it simple, and no gimmicks.

I'm trying to change the narrative of what it means to be successful, for a pizza shop and a food business, but also as a business owner and as an individual. When it's time, I'll tell my guys at the shop, I want you to have a stake in it. You guys grew up with nothing, I want you to have an opportunity to own something. You've helped build this. It's my dream that I can do this, and that they're interested in taking it on. Nobody was able to do this for me when I was coming up, so let me do this for them.

Most of us from the kind of places I grew up in don't make it. I'm proud to be from that environment. It made me. But I worked to go beyond that.

My parents' generation did whatever they needed to do to put food on the table. They're the ones who sacrificed so much for us to have something here. It's what pushed me to work hard and build a foundation that I want to pass on to the next generation, so I can motivate them to have more than what I've got.

And when I talk about our people, I'm not talking about just my personal people. I'm talking about everyone who comes from my world: the ones who struggle to make it and don't have the same advantages as others.

Our goal is for our people who come after us to do better than we've done. Otherwise, what's the point of all of this?

WHY WE DO WHAT WE DO

We got a lot of attention when people found out we were milling our own flour, but eating healthy wasn't new to me. People think everyone from the hood eats garbage, but that's not true. We all cooked in the house—and we were great cooks. We weren't eating like kings and queens all the time, but we were fortunate that we had food and knew how to stretch it.

From a young age, I always tried to eat as healthy as possible. I hung around a lot of Jamaicans, who have a long history of veganism and eating raw food. There are always Caribbean and African spots in the hood with natural foods, and they taught me not to drink soda, to avoid chemicals, and to use all-natural products. We've always known about this.

I've tried different ways of eating. I was vegan when I was younger, and I was even a raw foodist for a year or two. So I like to make sure there are options for our vegan and vegetarian customers at the shop. I've always been interested in learning about whatever makes food, not just pizza, taste good and be good for you.

When I planned to open Scarr's Pizza, I started researching flour from a health perspective. You know people can make fun, "Oh, you're bougie because you mill flour." But it's been a part of what we do from the beginning. And at first, we kept it low-key because I didn't want people to assume we were doing it for other reasons.

I mill the flour because I want it to be better for you. That's it. I want it to be as fresh as possible so you can keep all the nutrients in it. The fresher the flour, the more nutrient

dense it is. People have this association that pizza is empty calories, but it doesn't have to be.

The myth is that people think wheat bread, and bread that tastes noticeably whole grain, is healthy for you and that it has to taste like that. But I found out you can get rid of a part of the wheat berry that gives it that grainy, rustic flavor without destroying other nutrients.

I got a lot of inspiration read-

ing about French bakers. I always assumed the bread in Paris was way better because of the butter. But when I actually started getting into this, I realized it's the flour. It's stone-milled.

Learning about this really opened my eyes to thinking that we could do the same with pizza and make it not super wheaty.

I also talked to bakers I knew, like my friends Wendy and Rachel who had both worked at Tartine and have since moved on to do their own thing. They were doing stuff with bread, like milling their own flour and using different kinds of grains, that no one had done on a commercial scale.

At the time, I had also gotten into healthier breads. I don't remember how I got into them first, but once I

started reading and trying these different things, I got hooked.

I was reading about how bakers were experimenting with ancient grains. And I read about pizza guys working with regional wheat and doing interesting things with better ingredients for pizza. But everyone thought Neapolitan style was the best pizza at the time. It seemed like it was all tiny, expensive pies with ingredients that aren't necessarily for the everyday person.

And then it hit me. No one is doing this like how I want to do it here. It isn't an affordable price, and they're definitely not doing it with a slice joint.

We had the mill before we opened, and I was testing it out. I ordered different types of wheat berries, milled them into flour, and then tried them together in different combinations. Some combos or ratios worked better than others. At first, I was mixing red wheat with white wheat; the red was too wheaty for people. It took me months to figure everything out. I was ordering stuff, throwing it away, and trying again.

Actually, the first month of the shop being open, I was still milling all of the wheat myself—three different kinds for the flour blend. It was time-consuming and not sustainable.

There was a lot of trial and error, but luckily I figured it out. And now with our blend of flours from local mills and in-house, and the other ingredients I also picked out with a lot of testing, I proved that you can make New York–style pizza that's healthy.

WHEAT

When you mill wheat berries into flour, what you're doing is separating parts of the wheat berry.

BRAN: This is the fibrous outside shell, which is usually added back into what people think of as wheat flour and gives it that specific taste.

ENDOSPERM: This is the starchy inside stuff that makes up the majority of the weight of the wheat berry. It also makes up what people consider refined white flour.

GERM: It's the smallest part of the berry and contains the most nutrients. But it also has oils that die out and can go rancid quickly. Commercial mills usually separate out the germ for shelf life, losing all the nutrients in the process.

You can mill flour on a stone mill and then sift out the bran to refine the taste while still keeping the endosperm and germ. A stone mill doesn't get as hot as a metal one, which is what's used in most places for commercial flour production, so more of the nutrients in the wheat berries are preserved in stone milling. Buying wheat berries and milling them as fresh as possible, instead of buying commercial flour that may have sat on a store shelf for months, also helps retain more nutrients. Plus they keep for a really long time and take up less space than flour. But because freshly milled flour is less shelf stable, you'll want to use it within one or two weeks.

If you see the words *BLEACHED*, *BROMATED*, or *ENRICHED* on a bag of flour, avoid it. To make it white, manufacturers bleach commercially milled flour (which is already low on nutrients due to how it's processed), then they add chemicals to make it perform better (like potassium bromate, a known carcinogen)—and then they try to add back nutrients like niacin that are natural to wheat but lost during processing.

MILLING FLOUR AT HOME

The internal mechanics of all stone burr mills are essentially the same: a moving stone grinds a wheat berry or other grain or seed against another stone. But different countertop mills might work differently, so make sure to read the manufacturer's instructions on setup, use, and cleaning.

The recipes in this book recommend using 20 to 30 percent fresh-milled flour within the overall flour blend (see page 56 for more details).

Remember, you're sifting out the bran, which can be around 14 percent of the weight of the overall wheat berry, so measure out your flour for mixing dough *after* you mill and sift. You can weigh out the approximate weight in wheat berries, and add a little extra, then weigh out the flour again after you mill and sift.

For example, if you want 270g of fresh-milled flour for the standard Dough recipe with 900g of flour overall, start with 325 to 350g of wheat berries to be safe, mill the wheat berries, sift out the bran, and then measure out 270g flour from what's left. Whatever difference in flour you have, save for another use.

SIFTING

At our first shop, we started with a motorized flour sifter, which shook the flour back and forth across a screen, separating the bran. There are even mills with built-in sifters, so you can adjust how much bran you want to keep in your flour.

At home, you'll use a 40- or 50-mesh sifter or sieve (see description on page 48 for why). You're going to manually tap it back and forth across a bowl to catch the finished flour.

The more flour you have in the sieve at one time, the easier and faster it goes, since gravity will help do the work.

You can also use a coarser-mesh sifter to sift out the bigger pieces of bran first, then do one or two more passes with the fine-gauge sifter.

Some people will integrate some of the bran back into the dough during the final steps of kneading, before balling and proofing, to give it a stronger wheaty and nutty flavor. Personally, I don't like it for pizza. It also makes it a lot harder to stretch the dough as the bran absorbs more water.

If you are regularly milling wheat and want to save the bran, you can play around with it for other baking. Otherwise, compost or toss it.

TIMING AND STORAGE

I recommend milling the flour the day you plan to use it, but it's also OK to do it the day before. Whatever you mill at home is still going to be fresher than what you'll find in stores.

But because these nonindustrial stone mills don't separate out the endosperm and the wheat germ, which contains the densest nutrients, including oils that can easily spoil, you still need to use the flour relatively quickly.

You can store the flour in a container with an airtight lid and use it within a week or two for best results. Keep the container in a cool, dark cabinet or in the fridge.

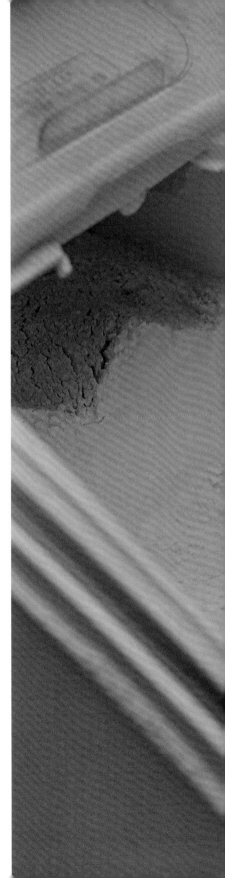

INGREDIENTS

There's no one out there who makes pizza that tastes like ours. It's the magic of our dough, made with freshly milled, organic flour, combined with our fresh tomato sauce, good cheese, and classic toppings.

I buy the best ingredients I can find: all-natural, organic, and local when possible. I'm serious about making pizza that tastes good and is good for you.

I also buy what I enjoy eating. We use boquerones at the shop instead of the more traditional anchovies because I like how the cure cuts through the cheese and sauce. And I personally don't eat pork, so we use all-beef pepperoni and make all-beef meatballs.

For home, find the best quality that's available where you live, or shop online. Play around with what's local. That's going to be the most interesting and is usually what tastes the best. Because we're in New York City, we use wheat from Upstate New York. But when I was in Tokyo for a pop-up, I made pizza with Hokkaido flour, and it was incredible. It had a different flavor profile,

more aromatic and lighter somehow, than what we get in the city.

There are some ingredients where it's unusual or just not possible to get locally, like olive oil. I love Greek olive oil, but I know it's traveling pretty far to get to the shop. If I'm choosing ingredients that aren't coming from nearby, then I'm definitely making sure I know who's producing them, if they use pesticides or not, etc.

Aim for minimally processed in what you use too. For our Cheese Blend (page 107), we buy different types of aged mozzarella and shred it ourselves at the shop. You can do that instead of buying the pre-shredded, bagged cheese at the grocery store, which usually has additives to keep it from caking.

Ultimately, I have a lot of strong opinions, but I don't have many hard rules about what I do or don't use, besides absolutely avoiding bleached, bromated, and enriched flour (see Wheat, page 39). But I'd say do your research, buy local whenever you can, and find out what tastes good to you—because what you're making is your pizza.

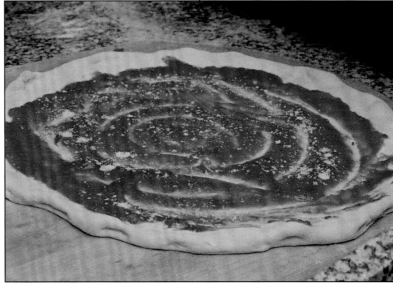

TOOLS

I highly recommend all of the tools listed here. It won't kill you not to have everything, and I make suggestions for alternative options. But there are a couple that you really need which I call out specifically.

THE ESSENTIALS

DIGITAL SCALE

This is necessary. It's ideal if it measures to the closest 0.1 gram. Measuring by weight will give you the best results, especially for the dough, where the ratios are really important to how well it turns out.

STAND MIXER

You'll want a stand mixer with the dough hook attachment and a bowl that's 4½ quarts or bigger to comfortably make the batch sizes in the Dough chapter. A stand mixer is worth the investment, and you can try baking other things.

Alternative option

I think mixing dough by hand is a waste of time, but I get that not everyone has a stand mixer. There's no secret, just more kneading. If you're mixing by hand, use the timing given as a general guideline and pay attention to the visual and physical cues in the recipe as the dough comes together. You may need to add a minute or two of extra kneading at each stage. See Mixing Round & Grandma Dough (page 64), for more tips.

BAKING STEEL

I don't want to endorse a specific brand, but look for the thickest available option, ½ inch if you can find it. Even when you aren't using it to cook pizza, it helps regulate the temperature of the oven. Make sure to check the manufacturer's instructions for preheating and cooking.

Alternative option

You can use a pizza stone if you want. Make sure to check the instructions on preheating and cooking. If you aren't sure if you want to invest in a steel or a stone yet, you can also use a big cast-iron pan (at least 12 inches in diameter) turned upside down or a half sheet pan. Like you would a pizza steel or stone, put the cast-iron or sheet pan in the oven while you preheat before cooking.

WOODEN PIZZA PEEL

This is something you must have. It's for building your pizza on top of and for getting it into and out of the oven. Since the recipes in this book are for round pies about 12 inches in diameter, look for a pizza peel that's at least 12 inches across and 14 inches long. (You can go a couple of inches bigger, but beyond that, it's hard to find space for it in an average home kitchen.) There are no real good alternatives for a wooden pizza peel. You need it to launch pizza properly. It's a necessity and an affordable investment.

METAL PIZZA TURNING PEEL

This is for handling the pizza, checking the bottom of the dough, turning it, etc., while it's in the oven. Something 8 or 9 inches in diameter with a handle that's a foot or two long is great. Just like with the wooden peel, you don't need something very big for home.

Alternative option

You can use two metal spatulas, one in each hand, instead. But it's nice to have a long-handled peel so you're not burning off your arm hairs in the process.

QUARTER SHEET PANS

These are ideal for baking Grandma and Sicilian pies at home. They're also useful for organizing ingredients or tools when you're cooking.

AIRTIGHT CONTAINERS

I prefer glass. These are for proofing dough and storing prepped ingredients. You want round or square containers that are both wide enough and deep enough for a dough ball to double in size. Food storage containers with locking lids work best. Tupperware or those round, flat to-go containers from takeout spots, with the black or white plastic bottom and clear lid, are great to reuse for this. You can also put each dough ball in a bowl—make sure it has enough room to double in size—then tightly wrap the bowl in plastic wrap.

OPTIONAL BUT NICE TO HAVE

UPRIGHT BLENDER OR IMMERSION BLENDER

Either one is key for making Pizza Sauce (page 94) and Vegan Vodka Sauce (page 96) extra smooth, as well as for making cashew cream or other dips, dressings, and sauces. A good upright or stand blender can be expensive, but it's unmatched in what it can do. For a lower cost option, an immersion blender is good enough for the sauces in this book.

FOOD MILL

I like the particular texture of milled tomatoes, smooth but not too fine. We start with canned whole peeled tomatoes, then mill them to make Pizza Sauce (page 94). But you can also use an immersion blender.

BENCH SCRAPER

They're inexpensive and helpful for portioning dough. I like metal ones, which work well for scraping dry flour off of boards. The silicone and plastic versions do the job too, and only cost a couple bucks.

COUNTERTOP STONE BURR GRAIN MILL OR GRAIN MILL ATTACHMENT

This is for when you're ready to go to the next level and mill flour at home. These days you can find small, countertop stone burr mills online starting at a few hundred dollars from companies like Mockmill. They even make versions that can attach to your stand mixer.

Look for stone mills only. You might find cheaper mills online with metal rollers, but you get what you pay for. Like I say on page 39, the benefit is that stone takes a lot of time to heat up, protecting your wheat berries from overheating and losing their nutrients.

SIFTER OR SIEVE

It's only necessary if you're milling your own flour at home. Look for a 40- or 50-mesh sifter, also called a drum sieve, to separate the bran from the freshly milled flour. The number refers to how fine the mesh is: 40 means there are 40 tiny openings per square inch; 50 means there are 50 tiny openings per square inch. The mesh needs to be at least this fine to sift out the bran for the ratios used in the Dough chapter recipes (page 55).

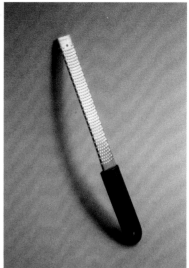

MICROPLANE GRATER
You'll want this for grating fresh pecorino romano and parmigiano reggiano onto the pies. It helps the cheese come out nicer, finer, and fluffier. It's a great tool to have in your kitchen in general for anything you want to grate fresh.

OVEN THERMOMETER
This is only if you want to get technical. It's a good way to figure out what temp your oven is actually at, how the temp changes when you take things in and out, etc. It can help you learn how to work with the oven that you've got. Personally, I prefer to do this by feel.

FOOD PROCESSOR
It's a pretty nice shortcut to be able to prep a whole head of garlic for Vegan Garlic Knots (page 156) or blitz herbs and panko for Meatballs (page 116). But not a big deal to have if you're just cooking at home and not scaling up recipes in a big way.

SQUEEZE BOTTLE
This makes drizzling olive oil easy. Or you can always put your thumb over the bottle opening.

PIZZA CUTTER
You can get away with a knife at home for slicing and serving, but a basic pizza cutter makes things much easier, especially with larger and heavily topped pies.

A FEW THINGS

This book will show you how to make the kind of pizza I like and the way I like to eat it—with the New York–style flavor profile and texture but healthier and with good ingredients.

Learning to make good pizza takes time, especially when it comes to getting to know the dough. The recipes and ratios are a starting point. That's the science. Learning to get a feel for the dough, to work with it by feel, to know what's wrong and how to fix it—that's more of an art.

But you'll get there with patience and practice.

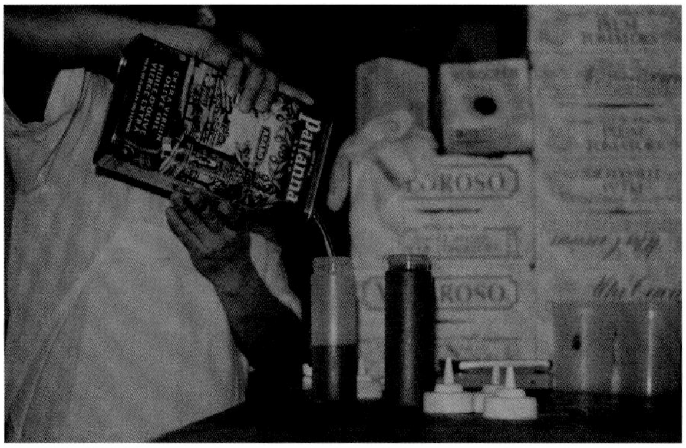

Think of this book as a guide. It has tips for common hiccups you might run into, general troubleshooting, and detailed photos. But every learning curve, and every pizza, is a little different.

It might take you a few tries, but you'll have fun doing it. And once you know how to make pizza like this, you'll always know. Knowledge is the greatest currency.

UNLESS OTHERWISE SPECIFIED:

Kosher salt is **DIAMOND CRYSTAL KOSHER SALT**. If you want to substitute another brand of kosher salt or sea salt you have on hand, measure it out by weight because different salts have different density. (For example, Morton kosher salt is almost twice as heavy as Diamond Crystal kosher salt.) Do not use iodized salt.

Black pepper is always **FRESHLY GROUND**.

Olive oil is always **EXTRA-VIRGIN OLIVE OIL**.

Water is **WATER THAT'S GOOD ENOUGH TO DRINK**—New York City tap water, for instance. If you want to use filtered water, go for it.

I like to use **COCONUT SUGAR** or other **LESS-REFINED SUGAR** rather than white granulated sugar. All of the recipes in this book were tested with coconut sugar or raw cane sugar.

Most recipes call for our **CHEESE BLEND** (a combination of two aged mozzarellas with different fat contents, page 107), sliced fresh mozzarella, or both. All recipes will specify what to use.

I recommend making dough with **FRESH YEAST**, also called compressed or cake yeast. You can also use active dry yeast. All of the dough recipes were tested multiple times with both fresh yeast and active dry yeast.

FRESH YEAST

The flavor of pizza made at home with fresh yeast is way better than with the dry stuff. It's richer and more multidimensional. Because fresh yeast doesn't go dormant the way dry yeast does, it activates more quickly and stays active longer, which is helpful for longer-fermented doughs.

Fresh yeast is not always easy to find, but it's worth getting. Look for it online or at well-stocked grocery stores in the refrigerated section. You can also see if your local bakery has it.

Just remember that fresh yeast expires faster. You might see an expiration date of only a week or two out from the date you're buying it. To extend its shelf life tightly wrap the block of yeast in plastic and freeze it. But if the smell or color of the yeast changes, throw it away.

If you need to, you can straight substitute the more commonly found active dry yeast by multiplying by 0.4. For example, the Dough recipe calls for 8g fresh yeast; you can use 3.2g active dry yeast instead. Add it to the recipe following the directions for fresh yeast.

TIPS

Most of the recipes in this book include both metric measurements by weight (grams) and standard US measurements by volume (tablespoons, cups, etc.). Especially when it comes to dough and baking, always weigh ingredients for the most accurate results. You can be a little more flexible with things such as seasonings for sauce or toppings, for example.

The recipes are based on what we do at Scarr's Pizza and what I like, but maybe you want your Vegan Vodka Sauce (page 96) a little spicier or your DJ CK Lemonade a little stronger (page 185). These recipes work, and I'll give you my honest opinion on everything else, but take what I'm giving you and make it your own.

When it comes to topping and cooking pizzas, all these combinations are inspired by what we do at the shop as well as other ideas I've played around with. But again, it's really up to you if you want more or less sauce, cheese, or whatever for any pie. However, be careful not to build too heavy of a pizza. It'll be hard to get it off the peel, especially if you're just starting out. (Check out the advice on how to top a pizza on page 75.)

All the recipes recommend baking at 550°F in a home oven with a pizza steel. But even then some things may need tweaking. Your oven might run colder than what you set, or the humidity and room temp, depending on the season and day, could be different. And the dough can also vary, even with foolproof recipes. It's a living thing. Use the timings given as guidelines but learn to keep an eye on your dough and your pizza and what they look and feel like at each stage.

If you don't have a pizza steel, you can use a pizza stone, sheet pan, or a cast-iron pan turned upside down (see full details in Tools on page 46). Make sure to preheat the oven with your item of choice in it.

Like I mentioned before, the pizza steel can live in your oven on the middle rack even when you're not cooking pizza. Make sure you preheat for one hour before cooking—even after the oven beeps and says the regular preheat is done—for the steel to fully heat inside and out.

Depending on your cooking surface and on how your oven acts, you may need to add a little time to each step.

If your home oven does not go up to 550°F, bring it up as high as it will go. You won't necessarily get the same rise in the crust and the tanned bottom, but you can still make a pretty good pizza. Try adding a minute or two to the recommended cooking time. You can also finish at the very end by broiling to get a nice browned top.

I'm not going to open a Pandora's box of hows and what ifs. I don't know how any given oven might work in any given climate, or how any pizza might cook with all of the possible variables. But I hope with some of this stuff here—and other advice I've included with specific recipes, especially in the Dough chapter—you're off to a good start.

Now you just have to do it.

GLOSSARY

COOKING vs BAKING

I use these interchangeably throughout: "cooking the pizza," "baking the pizza." This is everything that happens between your topped dough going into the oven and coming out as a finished pie.

FERMENTATION

Fermentation makes food delicious. When dough is fermenting, the yeast is eating up the sugars in flour and producing carbon dioxide and alcohol, creating flavor, and causing the dough to rise. Fermenting dough also makes it easier to digest, which is true for other foods also.

HERO

Hero refers to any kind of sandwich built on a long sandwich roll. Outside of New York, it's usually called a hoagie, grinder, or sub.

MOZZ

Mozzarella. Our shredded Cheese Blend (page 107) is made of two kinds of aged mozz, but the recipes that call for it will always say Cheese Blend. Recipes that call for fresh mozzarella, sliced or torn, will always specify fresh mozz.

ON LINE

In New York you wait *on line*, not *in line*. Saying you're "on line" is one way to tell if someone is a New Yorker.

OPENING THE DOUGH

This is the process of turning the dough from ball form into an opened up, stretched out, shaped, and ready-to-go round or square dough.

PEC and PARM

Short for pecorino romano and parmigiano reggiano. Pec is a little crumblier and saltier, and parm is a little sweeter. You can use them interchangeably in our recipes, whichever you prefer.

PIZZA vs PIE

A pizza is a pie, and a pie is a pizza.

PROOFING

Proofing is the final rise after dough has been shaped, but people often say "proof" or "proofing" for any stage when the dough is resting and fermentation is happening. Sicilian squares get an extra proof overnight.

THE SHOP

I say "the shop" when I'm talking about Scarr's Pizza.

SLICE PIZZA

Slice pizza is New York–style pizza that you buy by the slice at a counter-service spot.

DOUGH

At the shop, we make New York–style pizza using fresh, local flour that tastes great and doesn't have that whole grain flavor profile. We use our own blend: 30 percent flour we mill on-site from organic wheat berries mixed with 35 percent all-purpose flour and 35 percent high-gluten flour, both organic, grown, and milled in Upstate New York.

I highly recommend milling your own flour or buying freshly milled flour if you're lucky enough to live near a place that offers it. You really can taste and feel the difference. It's fresher, nutty, and both earthy and sweet.

We source the wheat berries to mill our own flour as well as the all-purpose flour and high-gluten flour from the largest organic flour mill in New York State. Search for what's close to you and try it out.

If you decide to use fresh-milled flour, play around with between 20 to 30 percent in your ratio, then make up the rest with equal parts all-purpose flour and high-gluten flour.

If you aren't using fresh-milled flour, you can use a 50:50 ratio of all-purpose flour and high-gluten flour. But always use local organic flour and any other ingredients as much as possible.

On top of sourcing and milling good flour, what really brings out the flavor in our dough is the long fermentation time.

Believe it or not, a lot of shops that keep to the basics make the dough and cook it the same day. There's very rarely fermentation. They pound it with yeast, and they add mad sugar to it—and people who don't know what goes into it think it's great because they get sweet dough, sweet sauce, and saltiness from the cheese. I know because I worked at those places.

You'll always get a much better flavor from using good ingredients and really taking the time to let the dough ferment. Give it at least one day, if not two or three days, to allow it to build flavor and create a stronger gluten structure.

People also have this idea that pizza has to be sour-dough for it to be healthy, and that's not true. It's the ingredients that you use that make it healthy and then allowing it to properly ferment. You can go all over the world to rural places with limited access and with people using the simplest ingredients, but they make these amazing flatbreads because they let the dough ferment for hours or days.

For all of the recipes in the book that involve dough, I recommend starting with dough balls that have rested in the fridge for at least 12 hours—and ideally 24 to 48 hours.

OUR DOUGH

This section gives you recipes for our Dough which you'll use for round pies and Grandma-style square pies, and also for Sicilian Dough, which you'll use for Sicilian-style square pies.

Each recipe is broken into four parts: Part I, mixing the dough; Part II, balling the dough; Part III, how to open, stretch, and shape the dough; and Part IV, the final step, baking. The general directions for mixing and balling will be the same or similar for whatever dough you are working with, but making the dough for rounds and squares will be different.

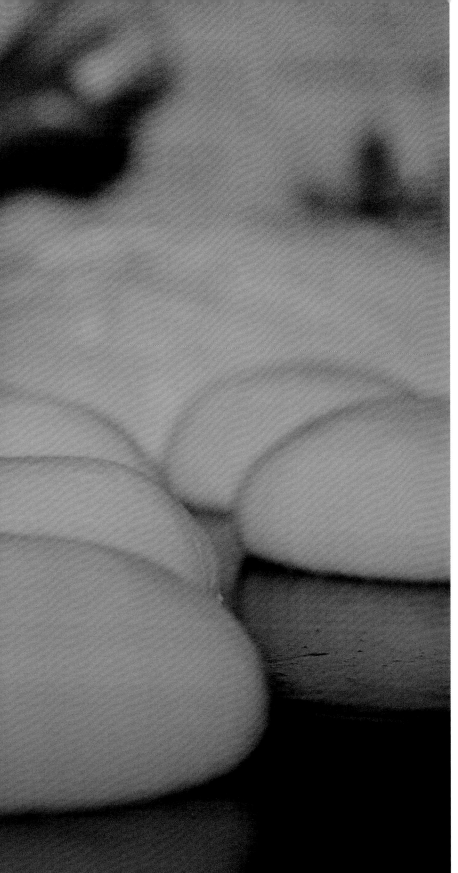

FLOUR BLEND

Here's my take on why high-gluten flour and all purpose-flour work together.

The high-gluten flour is what gives New York pizza its sturdiness and chew, because it has a higher protein content, around 14 percent, versus all-purpose, which is usually 9 to 11 percent, or even bread flour, which is typically 12 to 14 percent. (It's what people credit for good bagel texture and chew too.) It's made from hard wheat that's been grown in a cold climate.

Dough made with 100 percent all-purpose flour will feel softer and floppier than dough made with part high-gluten flour.

It's not my preference, but if you can't find high-gluten flour, you can try using bread flour with all-purpose flour in your 50:50 ratio, just to give at least a little bit of difference in protein content and sturdiness.

ROUND & GRANDMA DOUGH

My main goal is to have a good crust. That's the most important to me. I can live with a decent to OK sauce, and a lot or a little cheese. But whether I'm eating my own pizza or someone else's, and I'm talking especially New York slice pizza, the crust has got to be good.

When I talk about crust, I'm talking about the outer rim of the pizza that you reach for to pick up a slice. I want this outside crust to be crispy, light, chewy, and soft. But not too light. The bottom should hold up but have some give. If you're not used to it, you might find it too tough, but good slice pizza should fold and not be too floppy.

I love our texture. Honestly, it took me a long time to get our pizza to where it's at now. This recipe will get you there at home.

PLAN AHEAD

It helps to have a loose schedule for making pizza from start to finish—all the way from mixing the dough to cooking the pies.

If you want to bake on Saturday night, start the dough on Thursday night. Then pull the dough from the fridge 2 to 3 hours before you want to bake on Saturday. So if you want to cook pizza Saturday night at 6:00 pm, start the process at 6:00 pm on Thursday night and pull the dough on Saturday afternoon at 3:00 or 4:00 pm.

You can use the time the dough is coming to temp to make the sauce and toppings. Or since everything stores well, you can make the sauce and toppings the day before and pull everything out when you're ready to bake.

Each dough recipe yields enough dough to make three or four pizzas, or a couple of pizzas plus one or two of the sides from Extras (page 149), which can serve up to eight people—depending on how hungry you are. Scale up or down if you're making pizza for a group, planning for a half to a whole pizza per person.

THURSDAY, 6PM

Start the Dough

FRIDAY

Chill Time

SATURDAY, 3–4PM

Pull the Dough

SATURDAY, 6PM

Time To Cook

TIMING

About 30 minutes for the prep and mixing stage and 10 minutes for the balling stage, with 30 minutes of rest time in between.

After mixing and balling the dough (Parts I and II), it will need to ferment for at least 12 hours in the fridge—ideally 24 to 48 hours—then rest for 2 to 3 hours at room temperature before use.

MAKES

Makes 4 dough balls approximately 360g each, enough for four 12-inch round pies or four 13-by-9-inch Grandma-style square pies.

This dough can also be used for Vegan Garlic Knots (page 156) and Calzone (page 152).

EQUIPMENT

Digital scale
Stand mixer with dough hook
    attachment
Containers with tight-fitting lids
    for storage
Bench scraper (optional)
Wooden spoon or spatula
    (optional)

INGREDIENTS

2 tbsp | 25g sugar
Generous 2½ tsp | 8g fresh yeast
1¾ cups plus 2 tbsp | 450g _or_ 2 cups plus 3 tbsp and 1 tsp | 500g cold water (see Hydration and Water Temp on page 62)
6¼ cups plus 3 tbsp | 900g flour
3 tbsp | 30g kosher salt
2¾ tbsp | 36g olive oil, plus more for your work surface and for storage
All-purpose flour for opening and stretching the dough, and for your work surface

HYDRATION AND WATER TEMP

A ratio of 450g of water to 900g of flour results in dough at 50 percent hydration, while 500g of water to 900g of flour results in dough at 55 percent hydration. This small difference can really affect how the dough feels and behaves.

If you're a beginner, start with the 500g water measurement to get a more elastic dough. The dough with less water, or 450g, will feel tighter when you're mixing and balling it, which can be harder to get the hang of when you're just starting out.

With some practice, handling dough made with a lower hydration will get easier. You'll need it when it's hot and humid out—making a less hydrated dough will prevent the dough from blowing up when proofing. You should also drop the yeast down to 3 to 4g and make sure your 450g water is ice-cold to prevent overproofing. You can do this by adding ice to a pitcher of water half an hour before you plan to make the dough, then measuring from the iced-down water.

The instructions for mixing the dough (Part I) are divided into steps, with the total amount of water broken down, step by step, from 450g. Adjust the math if you're using 500g instead.

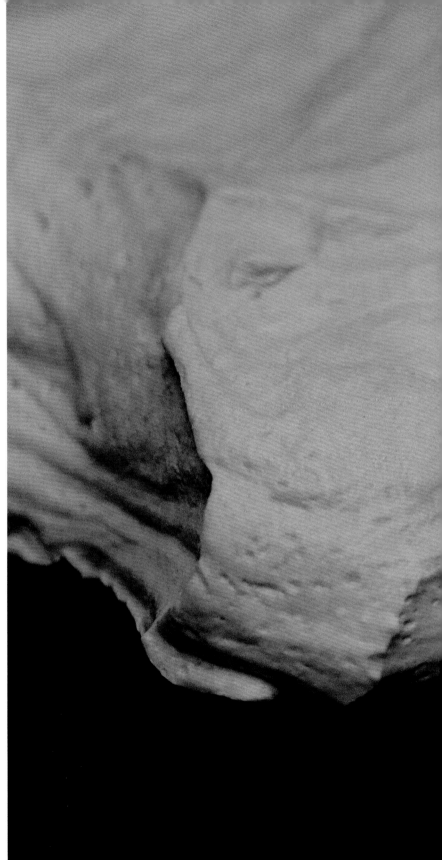

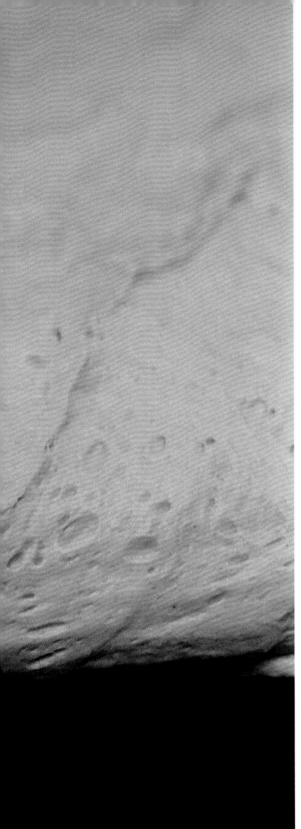

PROOFING

If you are baking with underproofed or overproofed dough, neither will rise enough and you'll end up with a dense and flat bake.

UNDERPROOFING

Underproofed dough won't have risen enough. This is most likely because it didn't have enough yeast, the yeast went bad, or it expired. Usually you just need to give the dough more time. The yeast needs to eat and process more, and the gluten structures need to develop further. If you've followed the recipe, including the recommended amount of proofing time, and  your dough ball hasn't expanded in size in its container, you can try letting it sit in its container in a warm spot for a few hours to see if it will rise before baking.

OVERPROOFING

You'll know if your dough has overproofed if it smells like beer or alcohol. This happens when the yeast has run out of food (or is close to it), produced too much gas, and the gluten structures have weakened. The dough will look slack and flabby. If you think your dough might be overproofed, you can try to save it by degassing it (punching down the dough to release the gas), reshaping it into a ball, and then letting it proof again back in its oiled container in the fridge. Check back on it in an hour.

If you find out during the baking process that your dough isn't properly proofed, it's too late. There's nothing you can do once it's in the oven. But it's good practice. If this happens to you, taste the dough anyway so you know what it tastes like when it's underproofed or overproofed. I would toss the rest of the dough, but if you don't mind how it tastes and don't want to waste it, you can turn it into bread crumbs or croutons.

PART I:
MIXING ROUND & GRANDMA DOUGH

1. In the bowl of a stand mixer, whisk the sugar, yeast, and half of the total water (225g) together until just dissolved.

2. Add the flour to the sugar, yeast, and water mixture. Set up the bowl on the mixer stand and insert the dough hook. Mix on the lowest setting for 5 minutes, until the sugar, yeast, and water mixture is absorbed into the flour. It should look soft and crumbly. I like to let the sugar, yeast, and some of the water get going before adding the salt.

3. Add the salt and mix at either the lowest or the second-lowest setting on the mixer for 3 more minutes, until the salt is thoroughly incorporated. The mixture should still look soft and crumbly at this stage and not too different from the previous step. You don't have to be super careful about when you add the salt, but some people think it risks killing the yeast if you add it too soon. Keeping it as a second step doesn't hurt.

4. With the mixer running at either the lowest or second-lowest setting, add half of the remaining water (112.5g) in a steady stream and mix for 4 to 6 more minutes, until the water is fully absorbed. The mixture will still look a little dry and crumbly but start looking more like a shaggy dough.

5. Usually at this stage—sometimes before, sometimes after—the dough may creep up the sides of the bowl. Or maybe, depending on the depth of the bowl versus the dough hook, the hook might have a hard time catching the dough. If this happens, you can pause the machine from time to time and use a wooden spoon or spatula to knock the dough toward the hook, then restart.

6. Especially for these first few steps, always keep the action low and slow, ideally between the first two speed settings of the mixer. If you mix too fast too soon, the dough will get tough. Feel the sides of the bowl and the actual mixer to make sure it isn't overheating. If it's very warm to the touch, or if you smell the oil from the motor, that's when you know you're overdoing it.

10. Be patient. If the dough is not coming together right away and it seems too dry, or too wet, give it another minute or two in the mixer. Do not add more water or more flour.

11. The final step before forming the dough into balls and resting the dough will smooth out a lot of the problems you might see when mixing. As the dough hydrates and the gluten structures begin to form, the dough smooths right out.

12. After you finish mixing, leave the dough in the bowl and cover the top loosely with plastic wrap or a cloth. Let it rest at room temperature for at least 20 and up to 30 minutes.

7. With the mixer running at either the lowest or second-lowest speed, add the oil in a steady stream and mix for 4 to 5 more minutes, until the oil is absorbed. You'll see the dough take on a slight sheen from the oil. At this point, it should really start coming together in a rough ball form. It should look and feel almost like stiff Play-Doh.

8. With the mixer running at either the lowest or second-lowest speed, add the remaining water (112.5g) in a steady stream. The dough will loosen up as you integrate the water, looking wet and slippery. Mix for 5 to 7 more minutes, until it comes back together and forms a clean dough ball, picking up bits of flour from the side of the bowl as it goes.

9. If you need to, you can take the speed up two or three notches without issue. You can try bringing it up to speed setting 4 or 5 (out of 10) if it feels like the final stage is dragging on and taking too long for the water to absorb. You'll see—and hear—as the clean dough ball starts to take shape and thumps or slaps the side of the bowl.

IF YOU'RE USING FRESH-MILLED FLOUR

I've fine-tuned these dough recipe ratios and don't want to encourage you to add more water or flour than what's written. Generally, I prefer working with a tighter dough.

But if you're milling at home and getting used to sifting out the bran, it might take a couple of tries to catch all of it. You'll see it as light tan specks. If you've got a lot of bran in the flour, it will absorb more water and make gluten development more difficult—and it'll be tough on the mixer to mix the dough.

If you find yourself with more bran than you want in your fresh-milled flour, but it's already accidentally mixed into the dough, you can still make it work.

If the dough is still in the mixer bowl, add more water to the bowl, 4 tsp | 20g at a time, mixing at low to medium speed until fully absorbed. Do this two to four times until the dough forms a smooth ball but isn't overly sticky or wet.

It might end up tasting wheatier than dough made with more finely sifted flour, but you will have something that's elastic enough to work with.

If you've already balled your dough and you're catching this when you're checking on it the next day, it's not too late—just annoying. The dough might look really tight and will not have changed much in size or smoothness. If this happens, take out the dough balls in their containers and let them come to room temperature. Working with one or two dough balls in the mixer at a time, add more water to the mixer, 4 tsp | 20g at a time, mixing at low to medium speed until fully absorbed. Repeat two to four times until the dough forms a smooth ball that's not overly sticky or wet.

Re-ball the dough according to the instructions on page 66, place the dough balls in their individual containers, and return the dough to the fridge.

PART II:
BALLING ROUND & GRANDMA DOUGH

HEADS UP

If you are trying out longer ferments—for 3, 4, or even 5 days—and working with fresh-milled flour, you might see black spots or speckles in the dough. That's normal and usually cooks out. The spots are bran particles that have absorbed water and oxidized.

If you want to avoid them, you can include a tiny pinch of ascorbic acid (vitamin C powder) in the dough when mixing. Look for it in drugstores and online.

1. After the dough has rested, give it a spin in the mixer for 30 seconds at medium speed (speed setting 4 or 5 out of 10). This tightens up the dough ball and makes it easier to cut. It should look and feel smooth.

2. Lightly oil your work surface with olive oil.

3. Release the dough from the mixer bowl, using your hand or a bench scraper to gently ease it out onto the oiled work surface.

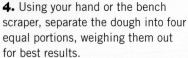

4. Using your hand or the bench scraper, separate the dough into four equal portions, weighing them out for best results.

5. Now, ball the dough. Working with one portion at a time, and with one side in each hand, pick up the dough and gently pull and fold the edges up toward each other into the center. Do this two or three times.

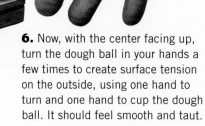

6. Now, with the center facing up, turn the dough ball in your hands a few times to create surface tension on the outside, using one hand to turn and one hand to cup the dough ball. It should feel smooth and taut.

7. Finally, crimp or pinch the center of the dough ball closed.

8. This is another way to make a dough ball, more or less the upside-down version of the first method: Place your portion of dough on your work surface, then round your cupped hands over it.

9. Using your fingers, pull and tuck the edges underneath toward the center, rotating the dough as you work. Do this a few times, always keeping the dough ball on the work surface.

10. Once you've got your smooth, taut exterior surface, turn the dough ball over and crimp or pinch closed the underside.

11. Lightly coat four containers with olive oil.

12. Each dough ball will need to go into its own separate container that is wide enough to accommodate it and deep enough to allow it to rise. I like covered containers with tight-fitting lids so the cold air doesn't affect the dough surface (see page 47).

13. Place the dough balls—closed side down, smooth side up—into the individual containers.

14. Close the containers if they have a lid, or tightly wrap them with plastic wrap.

15. Allow the dough to rest in the fridge for a minimum of 12 hours—ideally 24 to 48 hours for the best flavor—and a maximum of 4 to 5 days. When the dough is ready, it will have nearly doubled in size.

STORAGE

You can store the dough balls in their containers for up to 4 or 5 days in the fridge. If you are not using them within a couple of days, you can freeze them for later use, after the dough has first rested and then proofed for at least 12 hours in the fridge.

Working with one at a time, lightly coat each rested dough ball with olive oil. Wrap each ball tightly in plastic wrap, then freeze for up to 2 months. When you're ready to use, let the dough balls sit at room temperature until thawed. After they thaw, you can also unwrap them, then store them in oiled containers for 2 or 3 more days in the fridge if not using right away.

16. On the day you want to use the dough, pull it out of the fridge and let it sit at room temperature in its container for at least 2 to 3 hours and at most for 5 to 6 hours.

17. If you are trying to use the dough in less than 2 to 3 hours, leave the dough ball in its container and place the container in a warm place, like the top of a gas stove with the pilot lights on. Avoid placing the dough near AC vents or a fan. Do not put the dough outside. It's ready to use once it comes to room temperature.

TEMP CHECK

If it's a really hot day, the dough might come to temp in less time than usual. Keep an eye on it while it's resting on the counter in its container so it doesn't overproof and get too floppy and difficult to work with.

If it's a really cold day and the dough feels like it's resisting when you open it, let it sit and rest for longer to come to temp. Come back again in half an hour and try again.

DOUGH CHECK

After at least 12 hours of resting and proofing in the fridge, you can see if your dough is ready to work with.

The dough should have increased in size, ideally twice the size since you balled it. It should also look smoother and more elastic than when you first left it to rest.

To check if it's ready, press into the dough with your knuckle or a fingertip. It should dimple then spring back slowly, leaving a small indent. That means it's ready to open up.

If your dough does not pass the test, stick it back in the fridge and give it more time. The closer your dough is to being ready, the more it'll smell like bread. But if it smells like beer or alcohol, it might be over-proofed (see page 63).

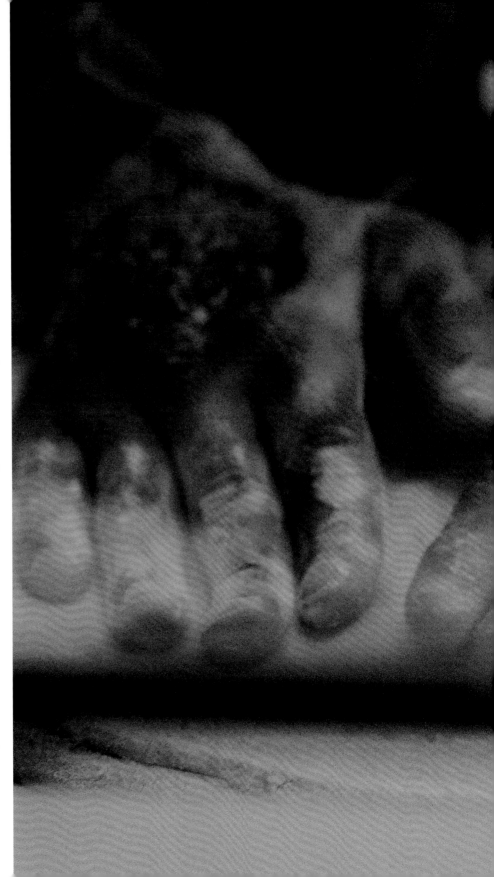

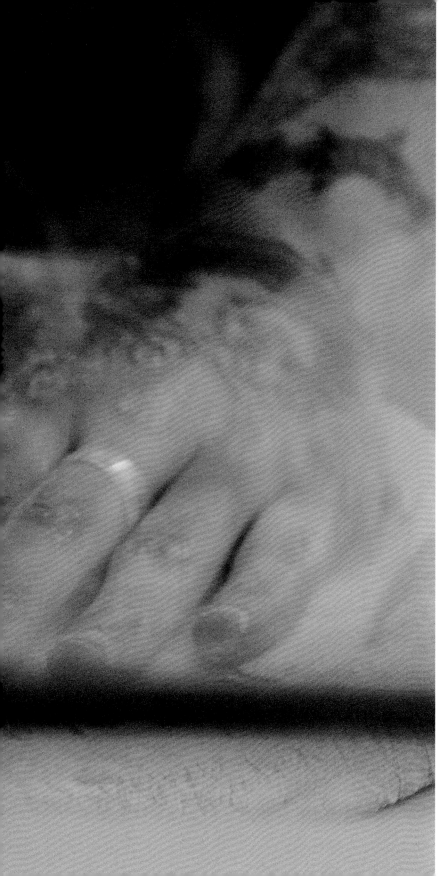

The next few sections will take you through opening up, stretching, and shaping round pies with the Round & Grandma Dough recipe, all the way to baking, or cooking, pizzas.

A REMINDER ON TIMING

Two to three hours before you plan to bake, take out however many dough balls as you want pizzas from the fridge. Let the dough balls come to room temperature in their containers on the counter.

One hour before you plan to bake, preheat the oven to 550°F with the pizza steel on the middle rack. Some home ovens won't get to 550°F, so preheat to however high your oven will go. Slide a rack into the top position too, for broiling.

OPENING ROUNDS

Everyone's got a different way of opening up the dough. I taught my guys at the shop how I do it, but they've each made it their own. Sometimes you'll use different techniques depending on the day and the dough, and this section lays out just a few go-to methods.

Patience is key to creating a really good pizza. Let the dough work for itself and you'll be good. It's that simple. I'm not saying take your sweet time with it, but chill and don't panic. Everything, for the most part, you can fix.

If you're struggling, bring the dough ball back together, let it rest for half an hour in its container on the counter, and then come back and do it over again. When you run into a problem, work backward, step-by-step, figure out what you did wrong, and then try it again.

After that, you'll never forget it.

PART III:
OPENING, STRETCHING, and SHAPING ROUNDS

1. Midway through the dough coming to temp—1 hour into a 2- to 3-hour rest on the counter—open the container, push down on the dough ball with your fist or palm, and close the container again to continue its rest. Pushing it down at this stage helps get rid of any gas that might have built up in its proofing. You're reducing air bubbles that can turn into thin spots when you open up the dough later.

2. Once the dough is to temp, lightly scatter flour over your work surface, smoothing your hand across it to make sure the flour is evenly distributed.

3. Fill a small bowl with flour. It should be big enough to fit the dough ball and hold enough flour to coat it. A wide, shallow cereal bowl with ½ inch of flour works great. Open the container with the dough ball. Transfer the dough ball to the bowl of flour and turn it over and around so it's lightly but completely covered. Brush and shake off any excess flour.

4. Flip your dough ball onto the work surface, keeping the original, smoother top side of the dough ball facing up. Firmly but gently, push down with your fingertips repeatedly all over the surface, forcing out any air bubbles.

5. Then, with one hand over the other, press your palms down on the middle of the dough, rotate the dough 90 degrees, and repeat.

6. You'll start shaping an approximately ½- to 1-inch rim. This rim will be your crust.

7. Now you are going to let gravity help you stretch out the dough. Pick up the flattened dough, about 6 to 8 inches in diameter, so the smooth side stays facing you, letting it hang down and touch the work surface. Rotate the dough, using one hand to feed it into the other—like you're turning a steering wheel. Do this a few times as the dough begins to stretch to about 10 inches in diameter.

8. Put your dough back down and press into it again with one palm over the other, fingers closed, in circular motions from the center outward, working toward the crust. Keep pressing, continuing to rotate your dough 90 degrees until you have a pie that is about 12 inches in diameter.

9. To stretch it out more, make two soft fists and slide your hands under the dough. Push your fists slowly outward at the edges of the dough. You want to open up and stretch the outside, not the middle or it will get too thin.

10. Drape the dough across the back of one hand and forearm, and use the knuckles of your other hand to stretch and push at the edges while guiding it over your stationary arm and hand—very slowly spinning the dough as it opens up. Continue, turning a few degrees at a time, until you've worked your way around the whole rim.

11. As the dough opens, you can hold it up draped over your hands just above eye level to check in the light for thin spots or thick spots.

12. If you catch a thin spot or hole, gather the dough on either side of the area and pinch it closed. For a thick spot, if the area is relatively large, repeat step 10 and keep working on it. For smaller areas, you can use two fingers to tug the dough gently in opposite directions to even out the thickness.

13. Lightly scatter flour all over your wooden peel. Make sure there is enough flour at the front, toward the lip, so the pie can slide right off, but not too much or it will clump together on the underside of the dough. Spread it around so it is evenly distributed.

14. Once you're close to the ideal size—12 inches—transfer your stretched dough to the peel.

15. Wiggle the peel from side to side and back to front to make sure the dough isn't sticking.

16. Check the edges for thick spots; you want everything to be even thickness. Gently use the pads of your fingers to slightly lift and stretch any thick or irregular sections as needed, running your fingertips under the edge of the dough and moving your hands away from each other.

17. Now you're ready to turn this dough into pizza. See Sauce (page 91), Toppings (page 101), and Pizza (page 121) for ideas.

PART IV:
BAKING ROUNDS

TIMING
About 15 minutes, from opening the dough through cooking.

One hour before you plan to bake, preheat the oven to 550°F with the pizza steel on the middle rack. If you don't have a pizza steel, you can use a pizza stone, sheet pan, or a cast-iron pan turned upside down (see full details in Tools, page 46). Slide a rack into the top position too, for broiling.

MAKES
Each dough ball makes 1 pizza.

EQUIPMENT
Pizza steel
Wooden pizza peel
Metal pizza turning peel
  (optional)

INGREDIENTS
1 ready-to-go pizza, opened up as instructed in the Opening section (page 70) and topped with whatever desired toppings from Sauce (page 91) and Toppings (page 101); see Pizza (page 121) for suggested combinations
Any desired garnish to finish (optional)

1. Turn the oven light on. You'll need to check for visual cues throughout the baking process.

2. With your topped pizza on the peel ready to launch, wiggle it again to make sure it can slide right onto the steel.

3. Once you open the oven door, immediately, in one low and fluid motion, guide the peel toward the back of the oven, just skimming the wood over the steel. You want to land your pizza right in the center. Once you're there, wiggle the peel and lift up and back as you slide the pie onto the surface. Just go for it and keep it moving at the same speed going in as coming out.

4. Within a minute, you'll see the crust puff up. After 2 to 3 minutes, reach in with your metal turning peel (or metal spatulas) and check the bottom. You want it evenly tanned and a little speckled. Once the bottom begins to firm up, use your metal peel to rotate it a quarter or half turn every minute or so, continuing to check the bottom.

5. After 4 to 5 minutes total on the steel, your pizza should be evenly browned on the bottom and the crust should feel firm. Transfer it to the top rack to finish baking for 2 to 3 more minutes. For a browner top, switch to broil for the last 1 to 2 minutes.

6. Using the wooden or metal peel, remove the pizza from the oven and land it on a wooden cutting board. Top the finished pizza with any desired garnish. Slice and serve immediately.

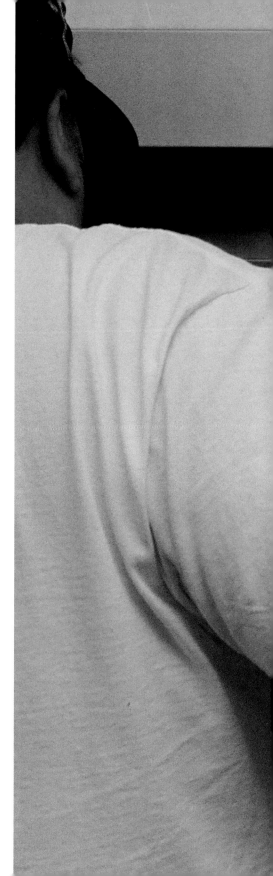

HOW TO TOP A PIE

Don't overtop your pizza or it will get too wet. Here are two techniques for saucing and then topping pizza.

For beginners, start by scattering a handful of cheese evenly on the stretched dough, then dollop a few tablespoons of sauce around the pie, spacing them evenly like polka dots.

You're working toward just shy of 1 cup | 100g Cheese Blend (page 107) and ⅔ cup | 150g Pizza Sauce (page 94) for a 12-inch pie. You may need less than you think. Everything will melt and stretch once the pie is in the oven.

This is a good way to get used to how much cheese and sauce a round pie this size can take without getting too heavy-handed and flooding it with cheese and sauce.

Once you get comfortable with that technique, move on to this, which is what I recommend in all the recipes in Pizzas (page 121): Ladle the sauce, one spoonful at a time, onto the center of the dough. Then take the back the ladle or a spoon and make circles from the center of the pie outward toward your crust. Top with cheese and desired toppings.

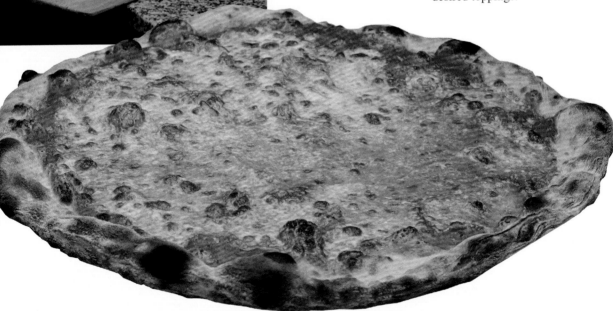

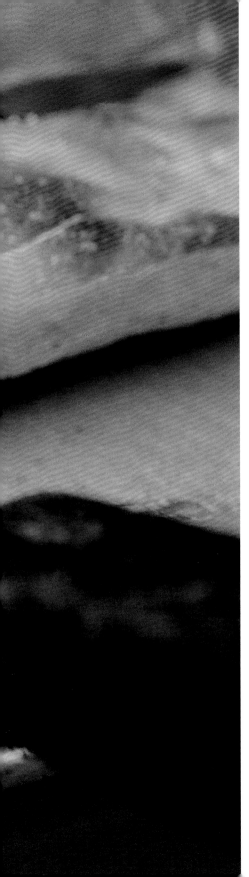

GRANDMA PIE

People love our squares. Of the two kinds of we serve, the Grandma style is a thinner, denser pie using the same dough as our rounds. After we stretch the dough in the pan for Grandma, we top it and cook it right away. Our other square, the Sicilian, has a more hydrated dough plus an overnight proof and is a fluffier, taller pie. The recipe and the method for that comes next, on page 80.

The trick for opening up the dough for Grandmas is to let it come to room temp and get really soft, to the point where you can stretch it to the edges of the pan without it shrinking back. Starting like the rounds, try to work with the dough after it's been out on the counter coming to temp for 2 to 3 hours. If it feels tight and not relaxed enough, let it rest some more. See the method for full instructions.

All of our Grandma pies at the shop come with sliced fresh mozz and shaved garlic, but you can top yours however you want. We build all the squares with cheese first, then sauce, and then toppings.

TIMING

About 15 minutes, from opening the dough through cooking— plus extra proofing time if needed.

One hour before you plan to bake, preheat the oven to 550°F with the pizza steel in it on the middle rack. You can slide the quarter sheet pan for the squares right onto the steel. (If you don't have a pizza steel, you'll slide the quarter sheet pan right onto the middle rack.) Slide a rack into the top position too, for broiling.

MAKES

Each dough ball makes 1 pizza

EQUIPMENT

Quarter sheet pan

INGREDIENTS

1 dough ball from Dough recipe (page 61), rested for at least 12 hours in the fridge—ideally 24 to 48 hours—then brought to room temperature
Olive oil for oiling the pan
Cheese, sauce, and any desired toppings
Any desired garnish to finish (optional)

MAKING GRANDMA PIES

1. Lightly oil a quarter sheet pan with olive oil. You want it barely oiled so the dough still sticks to some degree; too much oil and it's harder to make it stick to the sides of the pan.

5. Using all your fingertips, and working your way up and down lengthwise, lightly push down and outward on the dough until it is stretched the length of the pan. To help lengthen the dough, you can flip it over, work your fingertips up and down again lengthwise, and then flip it over again. Repeat until you've met the length of the pan.

2. Place the dough ball in the pan and gently flatten it out with your palm, pressing down once or twice. It's not really important how thick or thin it is, but what you're doing is pushing out any big air bubbles that may have formed while it was fermenting.

3. Loosely wrap the pan with the flattened dough ball in plastic wrap, and let the dough rest for another hour to relax further. On a warm day, it might be ready sooner; on a colder day, you may need to give it more time. You can check on it every half hour or so to see if it's pliable enough. What you want to be able to do is stretch it to all four edges of the pan.

4. When the dough is ready, remove the plastic wrap.

6. Now go for width. Again, using all your fingertips, press down on the dough outward toward the opposite sides of the pan until the dough evenly fills the entire pan, corner to corner. Run your fingertips under the far edges of the dough and lift, stretch, and press them up against the corners of the pan. If the dough still shrinks, let it hang out, covered, for another 30 minutes to 1 hour, then come back and stretch it again.

7. If the oiled pan is giving you trouble, you can also stretch the dough on a clean countertop, using the same techniques. Once you've stretched the dough to the desired size, gently peel it off your work surface and arrange it back in the pan.

8. Use a butter knife or your finger to dot all over the stretched dough, perforating the surface to ensure even proofing and baking.

10. Turn the oven light on so you can check for visual cues throughout the baking process. Bake for 8 to 9 minutes, until golden brown, rotating the pan from front to back halfway through the bake. For a browner top, transfer to the top rack and switch to broil for the last 1 to 2 minutes.

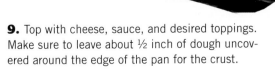

9. Top with cheese, sauce, and desired toppings. Make sure to leave about ½ inch of dough uncovered around the edge of the pan for the crust.

11. Remove from the oven and let cool for 2 minutes, then cut and serve.

79

SICILIAN DOUGH

The Sicilian is a whole other recipe from our rounds and Grandmas. The flour blend is the same, but the dough is more hydrated (at 65 percent versus 50 to 55 percent for the basic dough), and the technique is a little different. Sicilian takes an extra day of proofing, and it gets parbaked before getting topped and cooked off. This results in a higher rise, a fluffy, soft crumb, and an extra-crunchy bottom.

It's useful to have a schedule with this too. At the shop, we pull out the rested dough balls at night a few hours before closing, bring them to temp on the counter, then stretch, and keep them covered overnight in a baker's rack. We parbake the next day after about 14 hours of proofing.

Once they're cooled, we keep the parbaked doughs stacked up, ready to bake off throughout the day. You can follow our planning-ahead tips to create your schedule at home.

For mixing and balling, making this dough follows the same steps and time cues as the Dough recipe (page 61) but with different ratios of ingredients. You might find this wetter dough harder to form into balls, but if it gets stuck you can lightly oil your hands to make the dough easier to handle.

At the shop, we make our Sicilians upside-down style, with a combination of sliced fresh mozz and our shredded Cheese Blend (page 107) and with sauce and any toppings on top of the cheese.

TIMING
Like the Round Dough recipe, the Sicilian will take about 30 minutes for the prep and mixing stage and 10 minutes for the balling stage, with 30 minutes of rest time in between.

Also, like the Round & Grandma Dough recipe, I recommend making pizza with dough that has rested for at least 12 hours—ideally 24 to 48 hours—after balling.

MAKES
Makes 3 dough balls 475g each, enough for three 13-by-9-inch Sicilians, plus about 138g extra dough. The extra dough can be used to make Vegan Garlic Knots (page 156) or a small pizza.

EQUIPMENT
Digital scale
Stand mixer with dough hook attachment
Containers with tight-fitting lids for storage
Bench scraper (optional)
Wooden spoon or spatula (optional)

INGREDIENTS
2 tbsp | 25g sugar
Generous 1 tbsp | 10g fresh yeast (see note on page 51)
2½ cups | 585g cold water
6¼ cups plus 3 tbsp | 900g flour
3 tbsp | 30g kosher salt
1 tbsp | 13g olive oil, plus more for your work surface

WEDNESDAY, 6PM — **Start the Dough** → FRIDAY, 6PM — **Start Proofing** → SATURDAY, 8AM — **Parbake** → SATURDAY, 6PM — **Time to Cook**

PLANNING AHEAD

Since the Sicilian requires an extra overnight proof, add another day in your schedule. If you want to cook pizza on Saturday night, start by mixing the dough on Wednesday night.

Start your proofing process on Friday night after the dough has rested for 48 hours. For example, if you started the dough at 6 PM on Wednesday night, you can start the proof at 6 PM Friday night.

Parbake Saturday morning around 8 AM after 14 hours of proofing, then do the final cook on Saturday night. You can use the downtime in between to make sauce and toppings.

PART I:
MIXING SICILIAN DOUGH

1. In the bowl of a stand mixer, whisk the sugar, yeast, and half of the total water (293g) together until just dissolved.

2. Add the flour to the sugar, yeast, and water mixture. Set up the bowl on the mixer stand and insert the dough hook. Mix on the lowest setting for 5 minutes until the sugar, yeast, and water mixture is absorbed into the flour. It should look soft and crumbly, with parts of the dough beginning to clump together.

3. Add the salt and mix at either the lowest or the second-lowest setting on the mixer for 3 more minutes, until the salt is thoroughly incorporated. The mixture should still look soft and crumbly at this stage but shaggier.

4. With the mixer running at either the lowest or second-lowest speed, add half of the remaining water (146g) in a steady stream and mix for 4 to 6 more minutes, until the water is fully absorbed. It will start looking like a soft dough, coming together as a mass.

5. Just like with the Round & Grandma Dough recipe, if this dough is having a hard time coming together—you might see it rising up the sides of the bowl and the hook's path not catching everything—you can pause the machine and use a wooden spoon or spatula to knock the dough down back toward the center of the bowl to help get it back on the hook, then restart.

6. Especially for these first few steps, always keep the action low and slow, ideally between the first two speed settings of the mixer. If you mix too fast too soon, the dough will get tough. (Feel the sides of the bowl as well as the actual mixer to make sure it isn't overheating—that's when you know you're overdoing it.)

7. With the mixer running at either the lowest or second lowest setting, add the oil and mix for 4 to 5 more minutes, until the oil is absorbed. The dough will take on a slight sheen from the oil. At this point, it should really start to look like a smooth dough ball.

8. With the mixer running at either the lowest or second-lowest speed, add the remaining water (146g) in a steady stream. The dough will loosen up as you integrate the water, looking wet and slippery. Mix for 5 to 7 more minutes, until it comes back together and forms a clean dough ball, picking up bits of flour from the side of the bowl as it goes.

9. With this much hydration, the dough will be very wet and slippery at this stage. Take your time to bring the dough back together. Even when it's done, it may still be very tacky, soft, and stick to the sides of the bowl—especially in comparison to our Round & Grandma Dough, which is much tighter. That's OK. If it needs help coming together, bring up the speed of the mixer a few notches (speed setting 4 to 6 out of 10) and add a minute or two of mixing time.

10. After you finish mixing, leave the dough in the bowl and cover the top loosely with plastic wrap or cloth. Let it rest at room temperature for at least 20 and up to 30 minutes.

PART II:
BALLING SICILIAN DOUGH

1. After the dough has rested, give it a spin in the mixer for 30 seconds at medium speed (speed setting 4 or 5 out of 10). This tightens up the dough ball and makes it easier to cut. It should look and feel smooth. Then, using your hand or the bench scraper, portion into 475g dough balls. (You'll have enough for three dough balls; use the extra for a few Vegan Garlic Knots (page 156) or a small round.) Ball the dough using the same techniques as the Round & Grandma Dough recipe (see Part II: Balling, page 66).

2. Because this dough is more hydrated, it will feel smoother and softer, and is sometimes trickier—a little jigglier and stickier—to handle when balling. You can lightly oil your hands, your scale, and your work surface before cutting and balling the dough, so you don't lose any dough from it getting stuck to surfaces. Avoid adding more flour to your hands or surface when you get stuck because you don't want to add more flour into the dough itself.

3. This is also a larger dough ball, so you might find it easier to ball it on the counter instead of just in your hands. Try both methods and see what works for you. The most important thing is that you get the smooth, taut outside surface and that the bottom of the dough ball is completely sealed. Place the dough balls—closed side down, smooth side up—into their individual containers, close tightly, and allow the dough to rest in the fridge for at least 12 hours. When the dough is ready, it will have doubled in size.

STORAGE

You can store the dough balls in their containers for up to 4 or 5 days in the fridge. If you are not using them within a couple of days, you can freeze them for later use, after the dough has first rested and then proofed for at least 12 hours in the fridge.

Working with one at a time, lightly coat each rested dough ball with olive oil. Wrap each dough ball tightly in plastic wrap, then freeze for up to 2 months. When you're ready to use, let the dough balls sit at room temperature until thawed. After they thaw, you can also unwrap them, then store them in oiled containers for 2 or 3 more days in the fridge if not using right away.

SICILIAN PIE

The first few steps to making the Sicilian are very similar to making the Grandma pie. But you'll need at least 1 extra day or overnight to proof and parbake.

You should find it easier to stretch this dough versus the Grandma dough to fill the pan since it's a larger dough ball.

MAKES
Each dough ball makes 1 pizza

EQUIPMENT
Quarter sheet pan
Pizza steel (optional)

INGREDIENTS
FOR PROOFING AND PARBAKING
1 dough ball from Sicilian dough recipe (page 80), rested for at least 12 hours in the fridge—ideally 24 to 48 hours—then brought to room temperature
Olive oil for oiling the pan
2 to 3 tbsp tomato water

FOR COOKING
1 parbaked Sicilian dough
Cheese, sauce, and any desired toppings from Sauce (page 91) and Toppings (page 101); see Pizza (page 121) for suggested pairings
Any desired garnish to finish (optional)

TOMATO WATER

For the Sicilian, we use a technique (page 88) where we brush the dough with tomato water before proofing. We process canned whole peeled tomatoes for our tomato sauce. What we call "tomato water" is the thin liquid that remains after running the tomatoes through the food mill and reserving the milled tomatoes for sauce.

You can use the liquid at the bottom of a can of tomatoes for this, or you can thin out a little bit of sauce with water. The main point is to cover the dough lightly so it stays hydrated while proofing.

MAKING SICILIAN PIES

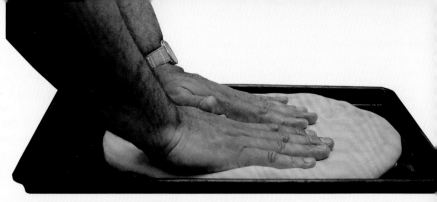

The day before you plan to parbake

1. Lightly oil a quarter sheet pan with olive oil.

2. Place the dough ball in the pan and gently flatten it out with your palm, pressing down once or twice. It's not really important how thick or thin it is, but what you're doing is pushing out any big air bubbles that may have formed while it was fermenting.

3. Loosely wrap the pan with the flattened dough ball in plastic wrap, and let the dough rest for another hour to relax further.

4. When the dough is ready, remove the plastic wrap.

5. Using all of your fingertips, and working your way up and down lengthwise, lightly push down and outward on the dough until it's stretched the length of the pan. To help lengthen the dough, you can flip it over, work your fingertips up and down again lengthwise, and then flip it over again. Repeat until you've met the length of the pan.

6. Now go for width. Again, using all of your fingertips, press down on the dough outward toward the opposite sides of the pan until the dough evenly fills the entire pan, corner to corner. Pull the edges of the dough and press it up against the corners of the pan. Run your fingertips under the far edges of the dough and lift, stretch, and press them up against the corners of the pan. If it shrinks, let it hang out, covered, for another 30 minutes to 1 hour, then come back and stretch it again.

7. If the oiled pan is giving you trouble, you can also stretch the dough on a clean countertop using the same techniques. Once you've stretched the dough to the desired size, gently peel it off your work surface and arrange it back in the pan.

8. Use a butter knife or your finger to dot all over the stretched dough, perforating the surface to ensure even proofing. Take a small amount of tomato sauce thinned with water—or the remnants of a can of tomatoes—and spread the equivalent of a few tablespoons across the dough, just enough to cover and help the dough stay hydrated while proofing (see Tomato Water, page 87).

9. Loosely wrap the pan in plastic wrap and let the dough rest at room temperature on the counter for 14 hours.

The day you plan to parbake

1. After proofing at room temperature for 14 hours, the dough should come up the sides of the pan and be proofed to the point where it might be touching the plastic. If the dough and plastic make contact, it's OK. Just be very gentle in peeling the plastic back so the dough doesn't get agitated and deflate.

2. One hour before you plan to parbake, preheat the oven to 550°F with the pizza steel in it on the middle rack. You can slide the quarter sheet pan onto the steel. If you don't have a pizza steel, you'll slide the quarter sheet pan right onto the middle rack.

3. Turn the oven light on. You'll need to check for visual cues during the parbaking process.

4. Once the oven is to temperature, slide the pan into the oven on the middle rack and bake for 8 minutes, until very lightly browned.

5. You're aiming for 60 to 70 percent done. At this stage, the dough should pull away slightly from the sides of the pan. It's ready when you cut it open and see a nice, even crumb. It shouldn't be gluey in the middle.

6. Let the parbaked dough cool, ideally an hour or two. Remove the dough and wipe out the pan. You can now use this parbaked dough to cook right away, or you can wrap it in plastic wrap and store it in the fridge for 2 to 3 days or in the freezer up to two months for later use.

When you're ready to cook

1. Preheat the oven to 550°F (1 hour before if you have a steel) with a rack in the middle position.

2. Generously oil a quarter sheet pan and place your parbaked dough in it.

3. Top with cheese, sauce, and desired toppings. Make sure to leave about ½ inch of dough uncovered around the edge of the pan for the crust.

4. Turn the oven light on. Slide the pan into the oven on the middle rack and bake for 8 to 9 minutes, until the cheese is browned, rotating the pan from front to back halfway through the bake. For a browner top, transfer to the top rack and switch to broil for the last 1 to 2 minutes.

5. Remove from the oven and let cool for 2 minutes, then cut and serve.

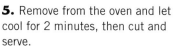

SAUCE

When I'm eating pizza, I look for the perfect balance of dough, sauce, and cheese. It seems simple, but it's not easy. And when you have all three working together you get the perfect product.

A good sauce is important in marrying everything together. It's got to be flavorful but not overpowering, savory but just sweet enough, without added sugar. We use tomatoes that are naturally on the sweeter side for our fresh, bright Pizza Sauce (page 94).

It's also a lesson in versatility. Make this main sauce, then always have it on hand. Besides for saucing pizza, it's a great base for other sauces, toppings, and sides, which you'll see as you keep going through this book.

PIZZA SAUCE

I like keeping the freshness of the tomato sauce. It doesn't get cooked until you're making a pizza, which gives it a brighter flavor.

Start with good-quality canned tomatoes, whichever brand you prefer. I like tomatoes that are naturally sweeter, and I also add a lot of fresh herbs and black pepper.

If you can't get fresh herbs or don't have time, dried is fine. Scale down to one-third of the amount if using dried herbs, since their flavor is more concentrated. Look for dried Sicilian oregano—it's more floral than other kinds of oregano.

Outside of pies, this sauce is great for simmering Meatballs (page 116) and is a foundation for Vegan Vodka Sauce (page 96) and Tomato Soup (page 173). You can also use the sauce for dipping Calzone (page 152) and Vegan Garlic Knots (page 156).

It keeps really well (see Storage note below), so even if you don't think you'll need what the recipe yields, make the whole thing and refrigerate or freeze the rest for something else.

TIMING
About 10 minutes

MAKES
Makes just more than 3½ cups or enough sauce for 5 or more pizzas, depending on how much sauce you use

EQUIPMENT
Large sauté pan
Immersion blender (optional)

INGREDIENTS
1 (28-oz | 794g) can crushed or whole peeled plum tomatoes, no salt added
¾ tbsp | 8g kosher salt
2½ tbsp | 32.5g olive oil
Generous 2 tsp | 7g finely chopped Vidalia or other sweet onion
3 garlic cloves, finely chopped
2½ tbsp | 6g fresh oregano, finely chopped
6 to 7 fresh basil leaves, torn
2¼ tsp | 5g black pepper

1. Combine the tomatoes and the salt in a large bowl and set aside.

2. Heat a large sauté pan over medium heat and add the oil. Once the oil is hot, add the onion and cook, stirring often, for about 1 minute, until translucent. It's just enough onion to cut the acid of the tomatoes.

3. Add the garlic, oregano, and basil to the pan and cook for 2 to 3 minutes, until fragrant.

4. Pour the contents of the pan directly onto the tomato mixture. Then add the pepper and stir everything to combine. If using whole tomatoes, blend until smooth with an immersion blender.

5. The sauce can be used right away.

STORAGE
Store in airtight container (preferably glass) for up to 3 to 5 days in the refrigerator or up to 6 months in the freezer. Refrigerated sauce can be used directly from the fridge. Frozen sauce should be left at room temperature until fully thawed.

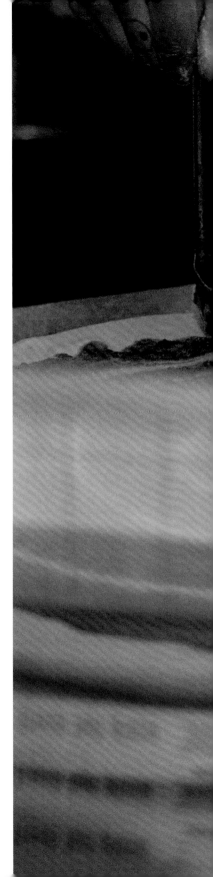

VEGAN VODKA SAUCE

I love the flavor and the silkiness of traditional vodka sauce, but the heavy cream doesn't work for people who can't handle dairy. And it obviously doesn't work for vegan folks.

Here's a version that builds on a cashew cream we make at the shop for other sauces and dressings. It's simple, blends well, and the coconut milk at the end gives it an extra-smooth mouth-feel and subtle flavor.

Feel free to adjust the amount of Calabrian chile according to how spicy you like your sauce. If you're using the whole chiles, chop them finely or blitz them in the food processor. If you're using the chile paste—especially if it's already blended with oil, vinegar, and other seasoning—taste it before using, then taste your sauce as it cooks so you can adjust accordingly. If you don't like it spicy at all, you can substitute high-quality tomato paste for that step.

The finer you chop the shallot and garlic, the silkier your sauce will be. If you want it extra smooth, you can also give the cooked sauce a minute or two in a blender.

Both the cashew cream and Pizza Sauce (page 94) can be made ahead, so pulling this together is easy.

TIMING
You'll need to soak the cashews for the cashew cream overnight (at least 8 to 10 hours) and have the Pizza Sauce made.

About 30 minutes, including making the cashew cream and cooking the sauce

MAKES
Makes about 3 cups, enough for several pizzas when combined with tomato sauce and toppings (see Vegan Vodka in Pizza, page 138).

The cashew cream recipe yields about 1½ to 1¾ cups, which is more than you'll need for the sauce. Reserve the rest for another use (see the Storage note on page 97).

EQUIPMENT

Large sauté pan

Powerful upright blender; ideally Vitamix or comparable; if you don't have one, you can use an immersion blender, but the results may not be as smooth

INGREDIENTS

FOR THE CASHEW CREAM
1½ cups | 195g cashews
¾ cup | 180g hot tap water, or more as needed to cover
Fresh cold water (optional)

FOR THE VODKA SAUCE
¼ cup | 52g olive oil, or more as needed
1 large shallot, minced
3 or 4 garlic cloves, minced
2 tsp | 10g minced jarred Calabrian chiles or Calabrian chile paste
½ cup | 118g vodka of your choice
2 cups | 450g Pizza Sauce (page 94)
1 cup | 227g cashew cream, or more as needed
2 tbsp | 29g coconut milk or your choice of nondairy milk, or as needed
Kosher salt and black pepper

The night before you make the sauce

1. In a bowl or a container with a lid, combine the cashews and hot water, adding more hot water as needed to make sure the cashews are covered; they will absorb the water overnight. Cover with a towel or lid and leave it on the counter until cool, then transfer to the fridge.

The day you make the sauce

2. For the cashew cream, add the cashews and their soaking water to an upright blender and blend until smooth, stopping and scraping down the sides as needed. Or, you can drain the cashews, rinse them with cold water, and then blend them with about ½ cup | 119g fresh cold water—accounting for the amount of water the cashews absorbed overnight—adding more water as needed. This results in a nicer, cleaner-tasting cashew cream. But the results are about the same.

3. Reserve 1 cup | 227g cashew cream for the vodka sauce and save the rest for a future use. Stored in an airtight container, it will keep for up to 3 to 5 days in the refrigerator.

4. For the vodka sauce, heat a large sauté pan over medium-high heat and add the oil. Once the oil is hot, add the shallot and cook, stirring often, for 1 to 2 minutes, until translucent. Add the garlic and cook for another 1 to 2 minutes, until fragrant and lightly golden. Make sure to keep moving the garlic and shallot around the pan so the garlic doesn't burn and turn bitter. Also make sure there's enough oil to comfortably coat everything. You

don't want the shallot and garlic swimming in oil, but they shouldn't be sticking to the pan either.

5. Stir in the Calabrian chile and cook, continuing to move everything, for about 1 minute, until fragrant.

6. Add the vodka and burn it off. Cook, stirring often, for 4 to 5 minutes to reduce the vodka, until the shallot, garlic, and chile mixture takes on a sticky, jammy consistency but still with some excess liquid in the pan. You'll smell the vodka bring out the fruitiness of the aromatics.

7. Add the Pizza Sauce and cook, stirring, for 1 to 2 minutes, until everything is integrated. Then add the cashew cream and cook, stirring, for 1 to 2 more minutes, until everything is integrated. The sauce will thicken and take on a warm orange-pink color.

8. To finish, stir or whisk in the coconut milk 1 tbsp | 14.5g at a time. Stir or whisk for 1 to 2 minutes, until the coconut milk is integrated and the sauce takes on a silky, glossy texture.

9. Season to taste with salt and pepper. The sauce can be used right away.

STORAGE

Store in one or more airtight containers (preferably glass) for up to 3 to 5 days in the refrigerator or up to 2 months in the freezer. Refrigerated sauce can be used directly from the fridge. Frozen sauce should be left at room temperature until fully thawed. The cashew cream can separate when it's frozen, so whisk or stir thoroughly before using.

TOPPINGS

You don't want to use too many toppings at once. If you order a slice, I'd say keep it to one or two. If it's a pie, three max. The reason being, if you overload a pie, then the toppings won't cook properly.

And people don't know this, but if you order more than three toppings, most pizzerias will give you the five or six toppings you want, but minimal amounts of each, so you're never going to enjoy it. Why have a few of a lot of toppings, when you can have a lot of a few? Do more with less.

In general, top your pie evenly, making sure that the heavy toppings don't weigh down lighter ones or cover them up and prevent them from getting crispy. If you're using sliced jalapeño or sliced garlic, for example, throw those on last.

If you're worried about your pie getting too heavy, wiggle it on the peel as you're building it to check. It should move easily on the peel so that later it can move off the peel into the oven. Add the cheese, check it, add another topping, check it, and so on.

If you're making a special pizza where all of these specific ingredients have to be a certain size or weight for the flavor profile to come together, that's different. But if you're just putting pepperoni and onions on a pie, you can eyeball the amount. No one's going to keep track.

But the best way to learn how to top a pizza is to make and top a pizza—and then do it again. Check out the general guidance and tips in this chapter and in

Pizza (page 121), but put what you want first. Adjust the amount after each try if you need to.

These are recipes for the toppings we make in-house. They line right up with our Dough recipe (page 61). So if you make one batch of Meatballs (page 116) or one batch of Cremini Mushrooms (page 108), then it's enough for at least four pies.

RICOTTA

At the shop we buy high-quality, whole-milk ricotta, then season and thin it for topping pizza. I learned this when I was working in another pizzeria. I never liked ricotta on pizzas back in the day because it was so dense and rich, but also bland for the most part. This pizza guy I was working with added black pepper and a little salt for flavor. And he taught me to whisk in heavy cream to make the ricotta light, airy, and silky—one of the best tricks ever.

TIMING
About 5 minutes

MAKES
Just more than 1 cup

INGREDIENTS
1 cup | 227g whole-milk
   ricotta
⅛ to ¼ cup | 30 to 60g heavy
   cream (or coconut milk)
   plus more as needed
1½ tsp | 5g kosher salt
1½ tsp | 3.5g black pepper

1. Put the ricotta, cream, salt, and pepper into a medium bowl. With a fork, whisk everything together until combined. Add additional cream if you prefer a smoother consistency.

2. To use as a topping, dot the ricotta across the finished pie with a spoon. You want it to warm up on the cooked pizza, rather than get baked in the oven. This way it stays nice and soft.

STORAGE
Store in an airtight container (preferably glass) for up to 3 to 5 days in the refrigerator.

CHEESE BLEND

You'll need this for almost everything. Start by looking for 1-pound | 454g blocks of mozz—not pre-shredded cheese—which should be available at most well-stocked grocery stores.

I recommend a blend of 70 percent low-moisture whole-milk mozz and 30 percent low-moisture part-skim mozz for an ideal pizza cheese blend that melts well and has great stretch and flavor. Using 100 percent whole-milk mozz tends to make the pizza oilier and greasier. But it's not a deal breaker and is still a better move to shred your own 100 percent whole-milk mozz rather than buying pre-shredded, bagged cheese, which has additives to keep it from caking.

1. Weigh out a ratio of 70 percent whole-milk mozz to 30 percent part-skim mozz for the amount of cheese blend you want to make. For example, for 4 cups | 400g of the blend, which is good for four pizzas, weigh out 10 oz | 280g whole-milk mozz and 4 oz | 120g part-skim mozz. Tightly wrap and refrigerate the rest of the cheese for another use (or to shred for the next time).

2. Using the biggest holes on the box grater, shred the whole-milk mozz into a large bowl.

3. Again, using the biggest holes on the box grater, shred the part-skim milk mozz into another large bowl.

4. Using your hands or a spoon, mix the 70:30 ratio of cheeses together until thoroughly blended. The blend can be used right away.

STORAGE
Store in an airtight container (preferably glass) for up to 3 to 5 days in the refrigerator.

TIMING
10 to 15 minutes

MAKES
You'll want about 100g (1 cup) shredded cheese for a plain pie or 80g (generous ⅔ cup) shredded cheese for a pie with cheese and toppings. So if you're making four pizzas with four dough balls from the Dough recipe (page 61), plan on at least 400g (about 4 cups).

EQUIPMENT
Box grater

INGREDIENTS
1 (1 lb | 454g) block low-moisture whole-milk mozz
1 (1 lb | 454g) block low-moisture part-skim mozz

CREMINI MUSHROOMS

Our mushrooms are thick and dehydrated—they're almost like mushroom jerky and look like meat on a pizza.

At most other pizzerias, even if they prep their mushrooms prior, they slice them pretty thin and sometimes throw them on top of a pie raw. There's not a lot of flavor when you do it this way. We season and roast it, which concentrates the flavor before you put it on the pizza.

I don't know why people throw out the stems. I think they're the meatiest part. Leave the stems on but trim off the very bottom where it might be woody or bruised.

TIMING
About 25 minutes for prep and baking

MAKES
About 1 cup

EQUIPMENT
Half sheet pan

INGREDIENTS
1 lb | 454g cremini mushrooms
Scant ½ tsp onion powder
Scant ½ tsp garlic powder
Generous ½ tsp black pepper
Scant ½ tsp kosher salt
Olive oil for oiling the pan

1.   Preheat the oven to 450°F.

2.   Rinse the mushrooms and pat dry. Trim off the very bottom of each stem, then cut the mushrooms into ½-inch-thick slices. Depending on how big your mushrooms are, you'll get three to four slices per mushroom.

3.   In a large bowl, combine the mushrooms, onion powder, garlic powder, pepper, and salt. Toss with your hands until the mushrooms are evenly coated with the seasonings.

4.   Lightly oil a sheet pan. Pour the mushrooms onto the prepared pan and spread in an even layer. Bake for 15 to 20 minutes, until the mushrooms are dark brown and have reduced by half. After the first 10 minutes, check the mushrooms periodically and move them around with tongs to make sure they are not sticking to the pan. When they're ready, they should be dehydrated but still juicy.

5.   Remove from the oven and let cool before using.

STORAGE
Store in an airtight container (preferably glass) for up to 3 to 5 days in the refrigerator.

ROASTED RED PEPPERS

Roasted peppers are easy to make at home and great to have on hand for everything. One of my favorite dishes at Ballato's is roasted red peppers with cherry tomatoes and fresh buffalo mozz. Emilio has done it like that forever.

I also like to eat roasted red peppers marinated with just balsamic vinegar as a side.

TIMING
About 25 minutes for prep and roasting

MAKES
About 1½ cups

EQUIPMENT
Half sheet pan

INGREDIENTS
1 lb | 454g red bell peppers, halved lengthwise, stems removed, and seeds scraped out
Scant ½ tsp onion powder
Scant ½ tsp garlic powder
Generous ½ tsp black pepper
Scant ½ tsp kosher salt
1 tbsp | 13g olive oil

1. Preheat the oven to 450°F.

2. Slice the bell peppers lengthwise into ½-inch-wide strips.

3. In a large bowl, combine the peppers, onion powder, garlic powder, black pepper, salt, and oil. Toss with your hands until the bell peppers are evenly coated with the seasonings and oil.

4. Pour the peppers onto a sheet pan and spread in an even layer. Roast for 15 minutes, until the peppers are soft and blistered.

5. Remove from the oven and let cool. Peel the pepper strips before using or storing. The skins should come right off. The peppers can be used right away.

STORAGE
Store the peppers, fully covered in olive oil, in airtight containers (preferably glass) for 3 to 5 days in the refrigerator.

BREADED CHICKEN

I don't believe in chicken on a pizza. At least not in my shop. But we make our own breaded chicken as the base for our Chicken Parm (page 165). It's also great roughly chopped for a salad topping. If you choose to put this on a pizza, that's up to you.

Making your own breaded chicken is always better than premade and frozen. Look for organic and free-range, and if you can go to your local butcher, even better.

For the best flavor, dry brine the chicken the day before. Sprinkle the sliced chicken breasts generously with kosher salt, about ¼ to ½ teaspoon per side, then refrigerate uncovered (on a rack on top of a sheet pan or large plate is fine) until ready to use. If you don't have a full day to prep, even brining the chicken for a few hours before cooking makes a difference in flavor.

TIMING
About 20 minutes prep time and 20 minutes frying time.

Plan for overnight inactive time if you're brining the chicken beforehand.

MAKES
4 to 6 chicken cutlets, depending on the number of chicken breasts

EQUIPMENT
Large cast iron skillet or
    frying pan
Meat mallet (or rolling pin)
Half sheet pan with a
    wire rack

INGREDIENTS
1 lb | 454g boneless, skinless
    chicken breasts
4 eggs
Scant ¾ tsp kosher salt
Generous ½ tsp black pepper
Scant ½ tsp onion powder
Scant ½ tsp garlic powder
½ cup | 80g rice flour, or more
    as needed
1½ cups | 90g panko, or more
    as needed
Neutral oil for frying

1. Working with one at a time, slice each chicken breast in half lengthwise to make two pieces out of each breast. Pat each piece dry.

2. On a clean work surface, using a meat mallet, pound each piece as thinly as you can. Each pounded piece should be about half the thickness of the original. For example, if the piece is 1 inch thick to start, the pounded piece should be about ½ inch thick. Set the pounded pieces aside.

3. Next, make the seasoned egg mixture. In a small bowl, whisk together the eggs, salt, pepper, onion powder, and garlic powder.

4. Set up the station for dredging and breading: one bowl with the rice flour, one bowl with the seasoned egg mixture, and one bowl with the panko. Have a clean sheet pan or large plate ready where your breaded cutlets can land before frying.

5. Working with one chicken piece at a time, dip it into the rice flour just enough to coat and shake off any excess. Next, dip it into the egg mixture, allowing the excess to run off, and then finally into the panko. Pat the chicken between your hands to help the panko stick and then shake off the excess. Set aside on the sheet pan. Repeat until all the chicken pieces are breaded.

6. Set a sheet pan topped with a wire rack or a large plate lined with paper towels next to the stove. Heat a large cast iron skillet or frying pan over medium-high heat. Pour in the oil to a depth of about ¼ inch and let it heat up. To check if the oil is hot enough to begin frying, stick the end of a wooden spoon into the oil. If small bubbles begin to form around the spoon, the oil is ready.

7. Work in small batches so the cutlets don't crowd each other in the pan. Shallow fry, turning once with tongs, for 2 to 4 minutes on each side, until both sides are golden brown. The timing depends on the thickness of the cutlets. Using tongs, land the fried cutlets on the wire rack to cool. Repeat until all of the cutlets are fried.

8. Slice or chop and serve hot on top of or alongside a salad, or make a Chicken Parm Side or Hero (page 165).

STORAGE
Store in an airtight container (preferably glass) for up to 3 to 5 days in the refrigerator.

FRIED EGGPLANT

It's key that the fried eggplant here is crunchy, not just as a pizza topping but also for eating in a sandwich or on its own. I love Japanese-style panko bread crumbs for this. They're airier and lighter. You can also use regular bread crumbs, which is a great way to repurpose stale bread. When we first opened, we would make our own crumbs using leftover bread from hero rolls.

Make sure that you're slicing the eggplant thin enough so it quickly cooks through and has a tender texture, but not so thin that you're mostly eating fried bread crumbs. We use the fatter, round Italian- or American-style eggplant, which is traditional, but you can use other kinds too.

We slice the fried eggplant coins in half for topping pizzas but leave them whole for the base of the Eggplant Parm (page 166).

TIMING
About 20 minutes prep time and 20 minutes frying time

MAKES
About 4 cups

EQUIPMENT
Large cast iron skillet or frying pan
Half sheet pan with a wire rack

INGREDIENTS
1 (1 lb | 454g) eggplant
4 eggs
Generous ½ tsp black pepper
Scant ½ tsp onion powder
Generous ¼ tsp garlic powder
Generous ¼ tsp kosher salt
½ cup | 70g all-purpose flour or 80g rice flour, or more as needed
1½ cups | 90g panko, or more as needed
Neutral oil for frying

1. Thinly slice the eggplant into coins about ¼ inch thick.

2. Next, make the seasoned egg mixture. In a small bowl, whisk together the eggs, pepper, onion powder, garlic powder, and salt.

3. Set up the station for dredging and breading: One bowl with the flour, one with the seasoned egg mixture, and another with the panko. Have ready a clean sheet plan or large plate where your breaded eggplant can land before frying.

4. Working with one eggplant slice at a time, dip it first into the flour, followed by the egg mixture, allowing the excess to run off. Finally, dip it in the panko. Pat the eggplant between your hands to help the panko stick and then shake off the excess.

5. Set a sheet pan topped with a wire rack or a large plate lined with paper towels next to the stove. Heat a large cast iron skillet or frying pan over medium-high heat. Pour in the oil to a depth of about ¼ inch and let it heat up. To check if the oil is hot enough to begin frying, stick the end of a wooden spoon into the oil. If small bubbles begin to form around the spoon, the oil is ready.

6. Work in small batches so the eggplant slices don't crowd each other in the pan. Shallow fry, turning once with tongs, for 2 to 3 minutes on each side, until both sides are golden brown. Using tongs, land the fried eggplant slices on the wire rack to cool.

7. Slice the eggplant coins in half if you're using it for a pizza topping, or leave whole if you want to make an Eggplant Parm Side or Hero (page 166).

STORAGE
Store in an airtight container (preferably glass) for 3 to 5 days in the refrigerator.

MEATBALLS

Every pizza shop should have meatballs. The key is the panade. Using the bread crumb–milk slurry makes the meatballs juicier.

A lot of people mix pec or parm into meatballs. At our shop, we use high-quality cheeses, and the flavor is strong, so we save our pec or parm for finishing along with olive oil, basil, and fresh sauce.

We fry the meatballs for a more consistent crust, then simmer them in a crockpot on the counter all day. We chop them up as a topping for pizza. They're also great for Meatball Parm (page 162). For sides and parms, you'll want extra Pizza Sauce (see page 94). If you're planning on serving the meatballs with sauce—versus chopping them up as a pizza topping—make sure to have a double batch of sauce on hand. You'll want the flavor of the fresh tomato sauce to eat with the meatballs, without the fat from the beef in the simmered sauce.

1. To make the panade, heat a large cast iron skillet or sauté pan over medium heat and add 1 tablespoon of oil. When the oil is hot, add the chopped onion and garlic and sweat, stirring often, for about 2 minutes, until translucent. Remove from the heat.

2. In a food processor, combine the garlic-onion mixture, the panko, parsley, basil, salt, pepper, onion powder, garlic powder, the remaining tablespoon of oil, and milk. Blitz for 2 minutes, until thoroughly moistened, but not wet; it should appear fluffy and springy.

3. In a large bowl, combine the beef and the panade. Using your hands, fold everything together until thoroughly mixed. Wash your hands after.

4. Line a quarter sheet pan with parchment paper for holding your meatballs. With oiled hands to prevent sticking, scoop out a few tablespoons of the beef mixture and cup and roll them between your palms to form a ball. At the shop, we weigh each meatball at 65g, but you can make them bigger or smaller. With this recipe, you'll get nine meatballs at 65g each, or about 2¼ oz, then one half-size meatball. Place each meatball on the parchment-lined pan as they're ready.

5. Set a sheet pan topped with a wire rack or a large plate lined with paper towels next to the stove. Return the skillet to medium-high heat. Pour in the neutral oil to a depth of about ¼ inch and let it heat up. To check if the oil is hot enough to begin frying, stick the end of a wooden spoon into the oil. If small bubbles begin to form around the spoon, the oil is ready.

6. Work in a couple of batches so the meatballs don't crowd each other in the pan. Shallow fry, turning the meatballs over every few minutes, for 8 to 10 minutes, until a crust forms on all sides and they are about 75 percent cooked. A meatball cut in half should still be pink in the middle. Using tongs, land the meatballs on the wire rack. Repeat until all of the meatballs are fried.

7. In a deep, heavy pot, like a Dutch oven, heat the Pizza Sauce over medium heat until just warmed through.

MAKES
9 to 10 meatballs

EQUIPMENT
Large cast iron skillet or large frying pan for frying meatballs
Food processor
2 quarter or half sheet pans
Heavy-bottomed pot for simmering meatballs in sauce

INGREDIENTS
FOR THE PANADE
2 generous tbsp | 27g olive oil
4 tsp | 13g roughly chopped white onion
4 or 5 garlic cloves, roughly chopped
1¼ cups | 75g panko (see note)
¼ cup | 3g loosely packed fresh flat-leaf parsley leaves
⅓ cup | 7g loosely packed fresh basil leaves
1½ tsp | 5g kosher salt
1 tsp | 2g black pepper
Scant 1 tsp | 2g onion powder
Scant ¾ tsp | 2g garlic powder
2 tbsp | 30g whole milk

1 lb | 454g ground beef
Neutral oil for frying and for oiling your hands
About 3½ cups Pizza Sauce (page 94) for simmering the meatballs, plus more for serving
Grated pec or parm, olive oil, and torn fresh basil leaves to finish

116

8. Add your meatballs to the warmed-up sauce, turn down the heat to low, and simmer, partially covered, for 1 to 2 hours, until the meatballs have softened in the sauce but still hold their structure and are not falling apart. At the shop, we keep the meatballs in a crockpot on the counter, ready to serve. At home, you can keep them on the stove for a few hours on low.

9. To serve on their own with sauce, pull the meatballs from the pot and plate them with a ladle of fresh sauce on top, plus grated pec, a drizzle of oil, and a few fresh basil leaves. Or use them for a Meatball Parm Side or Hero (page 162).

10. To use as a topping on pizza, chop the meatballs and crumble them across the pie. They're heavy, so go easy—and make sure to wiggle the peel to check that the pizza can still slide right off.

NOTE
You can repurpose 2½ oz | 75g stale bread for the panko. If you're doing this, tear the bread into pieces as small as possible. Then soak the pieces in the milk for 10 minutes to soften them up before using. If the bread is especially hard, add an extra 1 tbsp | 15g milk, but don't overdo it. The goal is to moisten the bread, not make runny bread crumbs. If you use panko, the panko pieces are so small there's no need to soak to hydrate them.

STORAGE
Store in an airtight container (preferably glass) for 3 to 5 days in the refrigerator. If making ahead, after frying the meatballs and letting them cool, you can freeze them in airtight containers for up to 2 months.

117

ITALIAN CHICKEN SAUSAGE

We make our chicken sausage in-house because no one really makes and sells one that's a good alternative to pork. This one tastes like a lighter pork to me, and a lot of people don't even realize it's chicken.

We use a mix of dark and light ground meat from our purveyor and spice it ourselves. Buy high-quality ground meat that you like. You can also ask your butcher to grind it for you. I prefer white-meat chicken in general, but using a mix of dark and light meat helps make sure there's a little fat in there to keep the sausage juicy and flavorful.

1. In a large bowl, combine all of the ingredients. Using your hands, fold everything together until thoroughly mixed.

2. To use as a topping on pizza, crumble or spoon the mixture raw directly on the pie.

STORAGE
Store in one or more airtight containers (preferably glass) for up to 2 days in the refrigerator.

TIMING
About 5 minutes

MAKES
About 1 lb | 454g

INGREDIENTS
1 lb | 454g ground chicken
¼ tsp kosher salt
Generous 1½ tsp | 3g red pepper flakes
2½ tsp | 5g fennel seeds
2 tsp | 10g olive oil

PIZZA

When you come to Scarr's Pizza, you'll always see classic New York pizzas on the menu, plus a few others with our own twists. Nothing bougie like figs and burrata though. Our pizzas use regular ingredients, like beef pepperoni and chicken sausage, but they're something unique.

We add dried oregano and grated pec or parm (pecorino romano and parmigiano reggiano, respectively; see Glossary, page 53) to every sauced pie, right on top of the Pizza Sauce (page 94), before our Cheese Blend (page 107) and Toppings (page 101). This gives it an extra layer of flavor that cooks into the sauce. Pec is saltier and crumblier than parm, which is a little sweeter. You can use them interchangeably here, depending on what grated cheese you prefer or have on hand to start and finish the pies.

I suggest grating the hard cheeses directly onto the pies using a Microplane or similar handheld grater. You

can also grate the cheese in advance, but I love that fresh shower of pec or parm. Avoid buying the already grated stuff if you can.

Since we make so many pies in a day we slice fresh mozz in thin, uniform slices on a deli slicer at the shop. At home, use a knife and aim for slices between ⅛ and ¼ inch thick. No need to do it in advance. And if you want, after you cut the slices, you can tear them into smaller pieces when you're topping your pizzas. Some cheese brands sell presliced fresh mozz, and you already know the answer: buy whole fresh mozz balls when you can.

Finally, we finish every pie except the Hotboi with more grated pec or parm and olive oil when it comes out of the oven.

Try these different combinations and see which ones you like best.

ORIGINAL

I love the simplicity of a plain pie. I'm a no-fuss guy. Simple man, simple pizza.

With a good pie, you're ideally getting the best of three things: the dough, the sauce, and the cheese. This is where it all begins. I don't mind toppings, but I've always liked doing the basics so I can really taste it. The bread can shine through, and it's not masked by other things.

Even when I go out and try someone else's pizza, I always try it plain. It's the best way to test if their ingredients are good. You can't hide behind three things. They're the holy trinity.

The Original is our most popular slice at Scarr's. I eat it all the time.

1.   Following the Dough instructions, open up the dough and stretch it into a 12-inch round pie (see page 70). Transfer the dough to a wooden pizza peel.

2.   Ladling the sauce one spoonful at a time onto the center of the dough, take the back of the ladle or a spoon and make circles from the center of the pie outward toward your crust. Make sure to leave about 1 inch of dough uncovered along the edge for the crust. Add more sauce as desired.

3.   Sprinkle the oregano and pec directly onto the sauce. Top evenly with the cheese blend.

4.   Following the instructions in the Baking Rounds section of Dough (see page 72), bake for 7 to 8 minutes total. Remember to

check the bottom, rotate the pie, and transfer it from the steel to the top rack when you need to.

5.   Pull the pizza from the oven and land it on a wooden cutting board or similar work surface. Finish with a drizzle of oil and more pec if you like. Slice and serve immediately.

STORAGE

Pizza is best eaten fresh. But if you have leftovers, let cool, wrap tightly in plastic wrap, and freeze for up to 2 months. Don't put it in the fridge. It keeps best when frozen fresh.

REHEATING

Follow the skillet method (see page 146) and reheat on the stove top. Or reheat in the oven or toaster oven.

TIMING

About 15 minutes from opening the dough through cooking.

To start, you'll need one dough ball rested for at least 12 hours in the fridge—ideally 24 to 48 hours—and then brought to room temperature.

One hour before you plan to bake, preheat the oven to 550°F with the pizza steel on the middle rack. (Some home ovens won't get to 550°F, so preheat to how high your oven will go.) Slide a rack into the top position too, for broiling.

If you're not using a pizza steel, preheat with your choice of alternative option (see Tools, page 46).

MAKES

One 12-inch round pizza

EQUIPMENT

Pizza steel
Wooden pizza peel
Metal pizza turning peel

INGREDIENTS

1 dough ball from Dough recipe (page 61)
⅔ cup | 150g Pizza Sauce (page 94), or more as desired
½ tsp dried oregano, or more as desired
1 to 2 tsp | 2 to 3g grated pec or parm, plus more to finish
Scant 1 cup | 100g Cheese Blend (page 107)
Olive oil to finish (optional)

MARGHERITA

Some people say you can't make a good margherita pizza with a gas oven, but they're wrong. This is our take on it, New York style.

Everyone expects the fluffiness of a Neapolitan pie when they think of a margherita. You can't replicate that with a gas oven considering Neapolitan pies are cooked in a wood-fired oven, and they're made of very refined 0 or 00 flour.

A margherita cooked in a commercial deck oven, like at the shop, or in a home oven with New York–style dough isn't bad, it's just different. Here, we pair the sturdiness and flavor of our crust with margherita ingredients. We keep it classic, with sauce and good-quality fresh mozz, and garnish with fresh basil at the end.

1. Following the Dough instructions in the Dough chapter, open up the dough and stretch it into a 12-inch round pie (page 70). Transfer the dough to a wooden pizza peel.

2. Ladling the sauce one spoonful at a time onto the center of the dough, take the back of the ladle or a spoon and make circles from the center of the pie outward toward your crust. Make sure to leave about 1 inch of dough uncovered along the edge for the crust. Add more sauce as desired.

3. Sprinkle the oregano and pec directly onto the sauce. Top evenly with the mozz.

4. Following the instructions in the Baking Rounds section of Dough (see page 72), bake for 7 to 8 minutes total. Remember to check the bottom, rotate the pie, and transfer it from the steel to the top rack when you need to.

5. Pull the pizza from the oven and land it on a wooden cutting board or similar work surface. Finish with a drizzle of oil and more pec if you like. Tear the basil leaves and scatter the pieces all over the pie. Slice and serve immediately.

STORAGE
Pizza is best eaten fresh. But if you have leftovers, let cool, wrap tightly in plastic wrap, and freeze for up to 2 months. Don't put it in the fridge. It keeps best when frozen fresh.

REHEATING
Follow the skillet method (see page 146) and reheat on the stove top. Or reheat in the oven or toaster oven.

TIMING
About 15 minutes from opening the dough through cooking.

To start, you'll need one dough ball rested for at least 12 hours in the fridge—ideally 24 to 48 hours—and then brought to room temperature.

One hour before you plan to bake, preheat the oven to 550°F with the pizza steel in it on the middle rack. (Some home ovens won't get to 550°F, so preheat to how high your oven will go.) Slide a rack into the top position too, for broiling.

If you are not using a pizza steel, preheat with your choice of alternative option (see Tools, page 46).

EQUIPMENT
Pizza steel
Wooden pizza peel
Metal pizza turning peel

MAKES
One 12-inch round pizza

INGREDIENTS
1 dough ball from Dough recipe (page 61)
⅔ cup | 150g Pizza Sauce (page 94), or more as desired
½ tsp dried oregano, or more as desired
1 to 2 tsp | 2 to 3g grated pec or parm, plus more to finish
3½ oz | 100g fresh mozz, cut into slices ⅛ to ¼ inch thick, then torn if desired
Olive oil to finish (optional)
4 to 5 fresh basil leaves to finish

VEGAN

We get a lot of vegan customers. And I've always respected vegan eating, so I wanted to make sure people had options when they came into the shop.

Our vegan original on the menu is a plain pie but with shredded vegan cheese similar to shredded dairy mozz, and people can add whatever toppings they want. By default, most of the veggie toppings we make are already vegan. Plus, we offer classics that are raw vegetables, like sliced jalapeños, shaved garlic, olives, cherry tomatoes, and sliced red onions, that get cooked on top. Do a combo of whatever you like.

At home, you can use the vegan cheese you prefer. Not all vegan cheeses melt the same, so follow the general baking guidelines using visual cues for the crust and bottom of the dough.

Like the non-vegan pizzas, you can layer in oregano and grated cheese on the sauce before you top it. Look for a hard vegan cheese that grates well like pec or parm.

These instructions are for making a vegan original round pie, but you can also make vegan squares. Refer to the Grandma and Sicilian sections in Dough (pages 78 and 88) if you're planning to do that.

1. Following the Dough instructions, open up the dough and stretch it into a 12-inch round pie (see page 70). Transfer the dough to a wooden pizza peel.

2. Ladling the sauce one spoonful at a time onto the center of the dough, take the back of the ladle or a spoon and make circles from the center of the pie outward toward your crust. Make sure to leave about 1 inch of dough uncovered along the edge for the crust. Add more sauce as desired.

3. Sprinkle the oregano and grated vegan hard cheese directly onto the sauce. Top evenly with the shredded vegan cheese and any desired toppings.

4. Following the instructions in the Baking Rounds section of Dough (see page 72), bake for 7 to 8 minutes total. Remember to check the bottom, rotate the pie, and transfer it from the steel to the top rack when you need to.

5. Pull the pizza from the oven and land it on a wooden cutting board or similar work surface. Finish with a drizzle of oil and more grated vegan hard cheese if you like. Slice and serve immediately.

STORAGE

Pizza is best eaten fresh. But if you have leftovers, let cool, wrap tightly in plastic wrap, and freeze for up to 2 months. Don't put it in the fridge. It keeps best when frozen fresh.

REHEATING

Follow the skillet method (see page 146) and reheat on the stove top. Or reheat in the oven or toaster oven.

TIMING

About 15 minutes from opening the dough through cooking.

One hour before you plan to bake, preheat the oven to 550°F with the pizza steel on the middle rack. (Some home ovens won't get to 550°F, so preheat to how high your oven will go.) Slide a rack into the top position too, for broiling.

If you are not using a pizza steel, preheat with your choice of alternative option (see Tools, page 46).

MAKES

One 12-inch round pizza

EQUIPMENT

Pizza steel
Wooden pizza peel
Metal pizza turning peel

INGREDIENTS

1 dough ball from Dough recipe (page 61)
⅔ cup | 150g Pizza Sauce (page 94)
½ tsp dried oregano, or more as desired
1 to 2 tsp | 2 to 3g grated vegan hard cheese
Generous ⅔ cup | 80g shredded vegan cheese of your choice that is closest in style to shredded mozz
Your choice of vegan toppings
Olive oil to finish (optional)
Grated vegan hard cheese to finish (optional)

HOTBOI

The Hotboi is one of the most popular pies in the shop—all-beef pepperoni, sliced jalapeños, and Mike's Extra Hot Honey.

This is an ode to the hot chile–infused honey made by our friend Mike. Other people make hot honey too, but his is the best.

We'll drizzle it on any slice for you if you're eating in, but this is the one pie where it's part of the recipe.

It's a simple, three-topping combination, where everything really works well together—the sweetness of the Extra Hot Honey contrasts with the savoriness of the pepperoni, and its sharp sting complements the fresh jalapeño flavor.

Our customers ask for the Hotboi in all styles, so instructions for all three are here: classic round, Grandma-style square, and Sicilian-style square.

INGREDIENTS

FOR A ROUND PIE
1 dough ball from Dough recipe (page 61)
⅔ cup | 150g Pizza Sauce (page 94)
½ tsp dried oregano, or more as desired
1 to 2 tsp | 2 to 3g grated pec or parm, or more as desired
Scant 1 cup | 100g Cheese Blend (page 107)
15 to 20 slices all-beef pepperoni, or enough to top the pie evenly
15 to 20 thin jalapeño slices, or enough to top the pie evenly
Mike's Extra Hot Honey (or similar chile-infused honey) to finish

FOR A GRANDMA PIE
1 dough ball from Dough recipe (page 61)
Olive oil for oiling the pan
3½ oz | 100g fresh mozz, cut into slices ⅛ to ¼ inch thick, then torn if desired
⅔ cup | 150g Pizza Sauce (page 94)
15 to 20 slices all-beef pepperoni, or enough to top the pie evenly
15 to 20 thin jalapeño slices, or enough to top the pie evenly
1 to 2 garlic cloves, peeled
Mike's Extra Hot Honey (or similar chile-infused honey) to finish

FOR A SICILIAN PIE
Olive oil for oiling the pan
1 parbaked dough from Sicilian recipe (page 80)
Generous 1 cup | 125g Cheese Blend (page 107)
1 oz | 28g fresh mozz, cut into slices ⅛ to ¼ inch thick, then torn if desired
⅔ cup | 150g Pizza Sauce (page 94)
15 to 20 slices all-beef pepperoni, or enough to top the pie evenly
15 to 20 thin jalapeño slices, or enough to top the pie evenly
Mike's Extra Hot Honey (or similar chile-infused honey) to finish

TIMING

About 15 minutes from opening the dough through cooking.

If you're making a round pie or a Grandma pie, you'll need one dough ball rested for at least 12 hours in the fridge—ideally 24 to 48 hours—and then brought to room temperature.

Or you'll need one parbaked Sicilian dough, either freshly parbaked and cooled or brought to room temperature from the fridge or frozen. (See Sicilian, page 80, for suggested schedule if you are making dough, proofing, parbaking, and cooking from start to finish.)

One hour before you plan to bake, preheat the oven to 550°F. (Some home ovens won't get to 550°F, so preheat to how high your oven will go.) If you're making a round pie on a pizza steel, or your pizza steel already lives in the oven, make sure it's positioned on the middle rack. Slide a rack into the top position too, for broiling.

If you are making a round pie but not using a pizza steel, preheat with your choice of alternative option (see Tools, page 46).

MAKES
One 12-inch round pizza or one 13-by-9-inch square pizza

EQUIPMENT
Pizza steel (if making a round pie)
Wooden pizza peel (if making a round pie)
Metal pizza turning peel (if making a round pie)
Quarter sheet pan (if making a square pie)
Garlic slicer (optional; if making a Grandma square)

HOTBOI, CONTINUED

For a Round Pie

1. Following the Dough instructions, open up the dough and stretch it into a 12-inch round pie (see page 70). Transfer the dough to a wooden pizza peel.

2. Ladling the sauce one spoonful at a time onto the center of the dough, take the back of the ladle or a spoon and make circles from the center of the pie outward toward your crust. Make sure to leave about 1 inch of dough uncovered along the edge for the crust. Add more sauce as desired.

3. Sprinkle the oregano and pec directly onto the sauce. Top evenly with the cheese blend.

4. Spread the pepperoni evenly across the pie, making sure the slices do not overlap too much for even cooking. Scatter the jalapeño slices over the top.

5. Following the instructions in the Baking Rounds section of Dough (see page 72), bake for 7 to 8 minutes total. Remember to check the bottom, rotate the pie, and transfer it from the steel to the top rack when you need to.

6. Pull the pizza from the oven and land it on a wooden cutting board. Finish with a drizzle of honey across the pie. Slice and serve immediately.

For a Grandma Pie

1. Following the Dough instructions, open up the dough and stretch it out in a lightly oiled quarter sheet pan (see page 78).

2. We're building this one upside down: cheese on the bottom, sauce on top. First, evenly layer on the fresh mozz, leaving about ½ inch uncovered along the edge of the pan for the crust.

3. Next, using a spoon or small ladle, drop dollops of the sauce on top of the pie, spacing them about 1 inch apart.

4. Sprinkle the oregano and pec directly onto the sauce.

5. Spread the pepperoni evenly across the pie, making sure the slices do not overlap too much for even cooking. Scatter the jalapeño slices over the top.

6. For Grandmas, we add fresh garlic too. If you're using a garlic slicer, shave the garlic as thinly as possible over the top of the whole pizza. Between 1 and 2 garlic cloves should get you 15 to 20 paper-thin slices, enough to top the pie evenly. If you don't have a garlic slicer, you can slice the garlic in advance using a mandoline or knife.

7. Following the instructions in Making Grandma Pies (see page 79), bake for 8 to 9 minutes total, rotating the pan from front to back halfway through the bake.

8. Remove from the oven and finish with a drizzle of honey across the pie. Let cool for 2 minutes, then cut and serve.

For a Sicilian Pie

1. Generously oil a quarter sheet pan and place your parbaked Sicilian dough into it (see page 89).

2. We're building this one upside down: cheese on the bottom, sauce on top. First, scatter the cheese blend all over the dough, leaving ½ inch uncovered along the edge of the pan for the crust. Evenly layer the fresh mozz on top.

3. Next, using a spoon or small ladle, drop dollops of the sauce on top of the pie, spacing them about 1 inch apart.

4. Sprinkle the oregano and pec directly onto the sauce.

5. Spread the pepperoni evenly across the pie, making sure the slices do not overlap too much for even cooking. Scatter the jalapeño slices over the top.

6. Following the instructions in Making Silician Pies (see page 89), bake for 8 to 9 minutes total, rotating the pan from front to back halfway through the bake.

7. Remove from the oven and finish with a drizzle of honey across the pie. Let cool for 2 minutes, then cut and serve.

STORAGE

Pizza is best eaten fresh. But if you have leftovers, let cool, wrap tightly in plastic wrap, and freeze for up to 2 months. Don't put it in the fridge. It keeps best when frozen fresh.

REHEATING

Follow the skillet method (see page 146) and reheat on the stove top. Or reheat in the oven or toaster oven.

MARINARA

This is basically a plain pie without the cheese and with double the sauce. I tell my guys to start with the normal amount of sauce (⅔ cup or 150g for a 12-inch round pie), then pull the pizza out halfway through the cook and top it with an extra serving of sauce. This lets the first amount of sauce cook in so you don't have it all pooling on the dough. It also builds multiple layers of tomato flavor, since you end up with longer-cooked sauce on the bottom and the fresher stuff on top.

The freshly shaved garlic and extra dried oregano also bring out those flavors that are already mixed into the Pizza Sauce when you first make it.

1. If you're making a round pie, following the Dough instructions, open up the dough and stretch it into a 12-inch round pie (see page 70). Transfer the dough to a wooden pizza peel.

2. If you're making a Grandma pie, open up the dough and stretch it out in a lightly oiled quarter sheet pan (see page 78).

3. If you're making a Sicilian pie, generously oil a quarter sheet pan and place your parbaked Sicilian dough into it (see page 89).

4. Start with half of the total sauce: Ladling the sauce one spoonful at a time onto the center of the dough, take the back of the ladle or a spoon and make circles from the center of the pie outward toward your crust. Make sure to leave about 1 inch of dough uncovered along the edge for the crust if making a round pie or about ½ inch uncovered if making a square pie.

5. Sprinkle the dried oregano directly onto the sauce.

6. Depending on your chosen shape, bake following the instructions in Baking Rounds (see page 72) or in Making Grandma Pies (see page 79) or Making Sicilian Pies (see page 89).

7. Halfway through the cook—3 to 4 minutes in—pull the pizza from the oven. Add the rest of the sauce, again ladling on the sauce one spoonful at a time and making circles from the center outward. Then, generously drizzle the oil all over the sauced pie, topping it evenly.

8. If you're using a garlic slicer, shave the garlic as thinly as possible over the top of the whole pie. Between 1 and 2 garlic cloves should get you 15 to 20 paper-thin slices, enough to top the pie evenly. If you don't have a garlic slicer, you can slice the garlic in advance using a mandoline or knife.

9. Return the pizza to the oven and finish baking, another 3 to 4 minutes.

10. Pull the pie from the oven, landing the round pie on a wooden cutting board or similar work surface and the square pie on a heatproof surface. Finish with more oil. You can also finish with some pec (or if you're trying to keep this vegan, some grated vegan hard cheese) if you like.

11. If it's a round pie, slice and serve immediately. If it's a Grandma or Sicilian pie, let cool for 2 minutes, then cut and serve.

STORAGE
Pizza is best eaten fresh. But if you have leftovers, let cool, wrap tightly in plastic wrap, and freeze for up to 2 months. Don't put it in the fridge. It keeps best when frozen fresh.

REHEATING
Follow the skillet method (see page 146) and reheat on the stove top. Or reheat in the oven or toaster oven.

About 15 minutes from opening the dough through cooking.

To start, you'll need one dough ball rested for at least 12 hours in the fridge—ideally 24 to 48 hours—and then brought to room temperature if you are making a round or Grandma pie.

Or you'll need one parbaked Sicilian dough, either freshly parbaked and cooled or brought to room temperature from the fridge or frozen. (See Sicilian, page 80, for suggested schedule if you are making dough, proofing, parbaking, and cooking from start to finish.)

One hour before you plan to bake, preheat the oven to 550°F. (Some home ovens won't get to 550°F, so preheat to how high your oven will go.) If you are making a round pie on a pizza steel, or your pizza steel already lives in the oven, make sure it's positioned on the middle rack. Slide a rack into the top position too, for broiling.

MAKES

One 12-inch round pie or one 13-by-9-inch square pie

EQUIPMENT

Pizza steel (if making a round pie)
Wooden pizza peel (if making a round pie)
Metal pizza turning peel (if making a round pie)
Garlic slicer (optional)
Quarter sheet pan (if making a square pie)

INGREDIENTS

1 dough ball from Dough recipe (page 61) or
   1 parbaked dough from Sicilian recipe (page 80)
2 to 3 tbsp | 26 to 39g olive oil, plus more for oiling
   the pan if making a square pie and to finish
1⅓ cups | 300g Pizza Sauce (page 94)
½ tsp dried oregano, or more as desired
1 to 2 garlic cloves, peeled
Grated pec or parm to finish (optional)

VEGAN VODKA

Vodka sauce is so rich and decadent. I love it on pasta—especially the version I make with cashew cream and coconut milk (page 96)—and wanted to see what it'd be like on a pizza. It's creamy, savory, and just the right amount of heat.

I didn't dream this up as a completely vegan pie because I like to add a little fresh mozz. But for a dairy-free version, you can try a vegan cheese that melts like fresh mozz. You can also make this a sauce-only pie and skip the cheese entirely.

1. If you're making a round pie, following the Dough instructions in the Dough chapter, open up the dough and stretch it into a 12-inch round pie (see page 70). Transfer the dough to a wooden pizza peel.

2. If you're making a Grandma pie, open up the dough and stretch it out in a lightly oiled quarter sheet pan (see page 78).

3. If you're making a Sicilian pie, generously oil a quarter sheet pan and place your parbaked Sicilian dough into it (see page 89).

4. You're going to sauce your dough in a few steps, alternating between Pizza Sauce and Vegan Vodka Sauce. As you work, leave about 1 inch uncovered along the edge for the crust if making a round pie or ½ inch along the edge if making a square pie. Using a spoon or small ladle, draw an approximately 1-inch-wide stripe of Pizza Sauce across the diameter of the pie. Next, draw an approximately 1-inch-wide stripe of Vegan Vodka Sauce alongside it. Go back and forth until you've covered the dough in the sauce stripes.

5. Next, evenly layer on the fresh mozz.

6. Depending on your chosen shape, bake following the instructions in Baking Rounds (see page 72) or in Making Grandma Pies (see page 79) or Making Sicilian Pies (see page 89).

7. Pull the pie from the oven, landing the round pie on a wooden cutting board or similar work surface and the square pie on a heatproof surface. Finish with a drizzle of oil and with grated pec if you like. Garnish with fresh basil leaves, whole or torn.

8. If it's a round pie, slice and serve the pizza immediately. If it's a Grandma or Sicilian pie, let cool for 2 minutes, then cut and serve.

STORAGE
Pizza is best eaten fresh. But if you have any leftovers, let cool, wrap tightly in plastic wrap, and freeze for up to 2 months. Don't put it in the fridge. It keeps best when frozen fresh.

REHEATING
Follow the skillet method (see page 146) and reheat on the stove top. Or reheat in the oven or toaster oven.

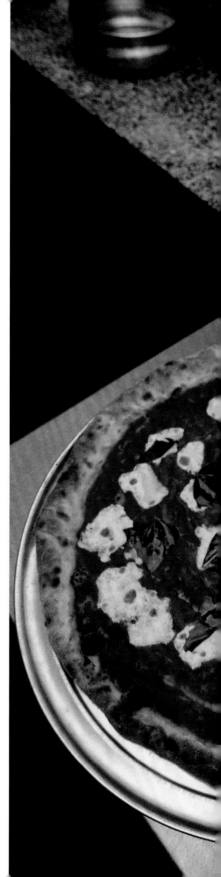

About 15 minutes from opening the dough through cooking.

To start, you'll need one dough ball rested for at least 12 hours in the fridge—ideally 24 to 48 hours—and then brought to room temperature if you are making a round or Grandma pie.

Or you'll need one parbaked Sicilian dough, either freshly parbaked and cooled or brought to room temperature from the fridge or frozen. (See Sicilian, page 80, for suggested schedule if you are making dough, proofing, parbaking, and cooking from start to finish.)

One hour before you plan to bake, preheat the oven to 550°F. (Some home ovens won't get to 550°F, so preheat to how high your oven will go.) If you are making a round pie on a pizza steel, or your pizza steel already lives in the oven, make sure it's positioned on the middle rack. Slide a rack into the top position too, for broiling.

If you are making a round pie but not using a pizza steel, preheat with your choice of alternative option (see Tools, page 46).

MAKES

One 12-inch round pie or one 13-by-9-inch square pie

EQUIPMENT

Pizza steel (if making a round pie)
Wooden pizza peel (if making a round pie)
Metal pizza turning peel (if making a round pie)
Quarter sheet pan (if making a square pie)

INGREDIENTS

1 dough ball from Dough recipe (page 61) or 1 parbaked dough from Sicilian recipe (page 80)
Olive oil for oiling pan if making a square pie, plus more to finish (optional)
½ cup | 75g Pizza Sauce (page 94), or more as desired
⅓ cup | 75g Vegan Vodka Sauce (page 96), or more as desired
3½ oz | 100g fresh mozz or vegan fresh mozz alternative, cut into slices ⅛ to ¼ inch thick, then torn if desired
Grated pec or parm to finish (optional)
5 to 6 fresh basil leaves to finish

DJ CLARK KENT

This one's for Clark, my OG. Not only is he a legendary hip-hop producer and DJ, he's also a great friend and my big bro. We even did a sneaker collab together. This pie is another thing we both kind of came up with together.

Growing up in New York, we all knew who DJ Clark Kent was. I met him for the first time when I was about eighteen. There was a Nike ID store on Elizabeth Street, and Clark used to be in there all the time. I don't remember what I said to him then. I don't like bothering people, but I probably said hi. We were just kids annoying someone we admired, but he was cool and friendly with all of us.

Over the years, my friends and I would see him at parties, stuff like that. Then after we opened I ran into him on Orchard Street where he was at an event a few shops down from us. We caught up, he started coming to the shop, and we've been close ever since.

We had just put a chicken sausage on the menu, and he'd never had it before. So I did a little combo for him. He likes it without garlic and I like it with. Make sure you shave the garlic on top after you've added the cheese, sauce, and sausage so it crisps as it cooks.

TIMING

About 15 minutes from opening the dough through cooking.

To start, you'll need one parbaked Sicilian dough, either freshly parbaked and cooled or brought to room temperature from the fridge or frozen. (See Sicilian, page 80, for suggested schedule if you are making dough, proofing, parbaking, and cooking from start to finish.)

One hour before you plan to bake, preheat the oven to 550°F. (Some home ovens won't get to 550°F, so preheat to how high your oven will go.) A pizza steel is not required for square pies, but if your pizza steel already lives in the oven, make sure it's positioned on the middle rack. Slide a rack into the top position too, for broiling.

1. Generously oil a quarter sheet pan and place the parbaked dough into it.

2. Scatter the cheese blend evenly all over the dough, leaving about ½ inch uncovered along the edge of the pan for the crust. Evenly layer the fresh mozz on top.

3. Next, using a spoon or small ladle, drop dollops of the sauce on top of the pie, spacing them about 1 inch apart.

4. Using your fingers, crumble or pinch off small pieces of the sausage and dot evenly across the pie.

5. If you're using a garlic slicer, shave the garlic as thinly as possible over the top of the whole pie. Between 1 and 2 garlic cloves should get you 15 to 20 paper-thin slices, enough to top the pie evenly. If you don't have a garlic slicer, you can slice the garlic in advance using a mandoline or knife.

6. Following the instructions in Making Sicilian Pies (page 89), bake for 8 to 9 minutes total, rotating the pan from front to back halfway through the bake.

7. Remove from the oven and finish with more oil and pec if you like. Let cool for 2 minutes, then cut and serve.

STORAGE

Pizza is best eaten fresh. But if you have leftovers, let cool, wrap tightly in plastic wrap, and freeze for up to 2 months. Don't put it in the fridge. It keeps best when frozen fresh.

REHEATING

Follow the skillet method (see page 146) and reheat on the stove top. Or reheat in the oven or toaster oven.

MAKES

One 13-by-9-inch square pizza

EQUIPMENT

Quarter sheet pan
Garlic slicer (optional)
Olive oil for oiling the pan, plus more to finish

INGREDIENTS

1 parbaked dough from Sicilian recipe (page 80)
Generous ½ cup | 125g Cheese Blend (page 107)
1 oz | 28g fresh mozz, cut into slices ⅛ to ¼ inch thick, then torn if desired
⅔ cup | 150g Pizza Sauce (page 94)
4 oz | 114g Italian Chicken Sausage (page 119), or more as desired
1 to 2 garlic cloves, peeled
Olive oil to finish (optional)
Pec or parm to finish (optional)

WHITE

This pie uses every cheese we have at the shop, so it's great for people who love cheese and also great for anyone who doesn't want tomato sauce. Given how rich it is with all the different cheeses, it's important to have plenty of freshly cracked black pepper, shaved garlic, and a bright, peppery olive oil as a finishing touch for contrast.

It's easier to build the White as a square pie because all the cheeses weigh down the whole thing. With a Grandma or a Sicilian, you can build everything right in the pan and don't have to worry about getting the pie off a peel. The crunchiness of the square as a contrast to the toppings is nice too. Don't be tempted to put too much cheese on this pie. The amount given for each will work just fine, since they'll all melt into one another as the pie cooks.

A white pie is supposed to look white, so the trick is the order you add the cheeses and other ingredients, which affects the look as well as the taste and texture. Start with shredded Cheese Blend (page 107) as the base; otherwise, this cheese can look too yellow when it melts. Also, the blend combined with the fresh mozz gives you a nice, stretchy cheese pull with each bite. With all the other pies I suggest adding the ricotta after the pie comes out of the oven, but for this one, you want to cook the pizza with the ricotta, so it bakes and mixes into the other cheeses. The shaved garlic on top also turns into an almost-translucent, melt-in-your-mouth garlic confit instead of crisping up, thanks to the fat and moisture from the cheese.

Like all the pies in this chapter, feel free to finish the last minute or two in the oven on broil for a slightly browner top.

1. For a Grandma, follow the Dough instructions, open up your dough and stretch it in a lightly oiled quarter sheet pan (see page 78). Or if you're making a Sicilian, generously oil a quarter sheet pan and place your parbaked Sicilian dough into it (see page 89).

2. Scatter the cheese blend evenly on the pie, corner to corner, leaving about ½ inch uncovered along the edge of the pan for the crust. Next, layer on the fresh mozz so it's evenly spaced across the pie.

3. Using the back of a spoon, dot the pie with ricotta in dollops about 1 inch apart. You can also spoon the ricotta into a piping bag—a plastic zip bag with one bottom corner cut off also works—and pipe it in even stripes or zigzags across the pizza for more even distribution.

4. Sprinkle the oregano evenly over the layers of cheese.

5. Next, generously crack fresh black pepper over the pie. At the shop, we use a lot of pepper for extra bite. If this is too spicy or not your preference, go a little easier.

6. Drizzle the oil across the topped pie, then sprinkle on the pec.

7. If you're using a garlic slicer, shave the garlic as thinly as possible over the top of the whole pie. Between 1 and 2 garlic cloves should get you 15 to 20 paper-thin slices, enough to top the pie evenly. If you don't have a garlic slicer, you can slice the garlic in advance using a mandoline or knife.

8. Following the instructions for Making Grandma Pies (see page 79) or Making Sicilian Pies (see page 89), bake for 8 to

9 minutes total, rotating the pan from front to back halfway through the bake.

9. Remove from the oven. You can finish with a drizzle of oil and more pec if you like, but it should be ready to go, since it's already been generously topped with oil and grated cheese. Let the pizza cool for 2 minutes, then cut and serve.

STORAGE
Pizza is best eaten fresh. But if you have leftovers, let cool, wrap tightly in plastic wrap, and freeze for up to 2 months. Don't put it in the fridge. It keeps best when frozen fresh.

REHEATING
Follow the skillet method (see page 146) and reheat on the stove top. Or reheat in the oven or toaster oven.

TIMING

About 15 minutes from opening the dough—or topping a parbaked dough—through cooking.

To start, you'll need one dough ball rested for at least 12 hours in the fridge—ideally 24 to 48 hours—and then brought to room temperature if you are making a Grandma pie.

Or you'll need one parbaked Sicilian dough, either freshly parbaked and cooled or brought to room temperature from the fridge or frozen. (See Sicilian, page 80, for suggested schedule if you are making dough, proofing, parbaking, and cooking from start to finish.)

One hour before you plan to bake, preheat the oven to 550°F. (Some home ovens won't get to 550°F, so preheat to how high your oven will go.) A pizza steel is not required for square pies, but if your pizza steel already lives in the oven, make sure it's positioned on the middle rack. Slide a rack into the top position too, for broiling.

MAKES

One 13-by-9-inch square pizza

EQUIPMENT

Quarter sheet pan
Garlic slicer (optional)

INGREDIENTS

1 dough ball from Dough recipe (page 61) or 1 parbaked dough from Sicilian recipe (page 80)

1 to 2 tbsp | 13 to 26g olive oil, plus more for oiling the pan and to finish (optional)

1 cup | 100g Cheese Blend (page 107)

3½ oz | 100g fresh mozz, cut into slices ⅛ to ¼ inch thick, then torn if desired

Scant ½ cup | 100g Ricotta (page 104)

½ tsp dried oregano, or more as desired

Black pepper

1 to 2 tbsp | 5 to 10g grated pec or parm, plus more to finish (optional)

1 to 2 garlic cloves, peeled

REHEATING PIZZA

To me, this is the best way to reheat a slice. It's also the fastest and you don't have to spend all that energy heating up the oven for a couple of pieces.

Use a cast-iron skillet with a lid big enough to hold your slice or slices. Place over high heat, add just enough olive oil to coat the bottom lightly (you're not frying, just lightly toasting), and top with the lid.

When the skillet is hot (after about 2 minutes), uncover and add the pizza slice or slices. After a minute or so when the bottom of the slice or slices begin to warm and recrisp, add an ice cube to the pan. Or you can also carefully drizzle 1 teaspoon water into the pan.

Re-cover the skillet, lower the heat to medium, and cook for a minute or two, until the cheese has melted. The ice will evaporate, creating a steamy environment so that the cheese and toppings don't dry out while the bottom stays crispy.

Plate and eat immediately.

ALTERNATIVE METHOD

If you're heating up several slices or a whole pie, you can use your oven or toaster oven.

Preheat the oven or toaster oven to 350°F with a rack in the middle position. If you're using a conventional oven and a pizza steel, put the pizza steel on the rack and preheat for 1 hour. When the oven is ready, put the slices or the pie directly on the steel. If you're not using a steel, put the slices or the pie directly on the rack in either the oven or toaster oven. If you're worried about cheese or sauce dripping through the rack, put a sheet pan on the rack directly below the middle rack to catch the drips.

Bake for 9 to 10 minutes, until the bottom is firmed up and the cheese is melted.

Plate and eat immediately.

146

SAUCE TO CHEESE RATIO

Use this rough guideline for how much sauce and cheese you should use on a pizza. You'll want a little less cheese for topped pies to make room for the toppings.

FOR EACH 12-INCH ROUND PLAIN PIE:

⅔ cup | 150g sauce
+
Scant 1 cup | 100g cheese blend

FOR EACH GRANDMA PLAIN PIE:

⅔ cup | 150g sauce
+
3½ oz | 100g fresh mozz

FOR EACH SICILIAN PLAIN PIE:

⅔ cup | 150g sauce
+
Scant 1½ cups | 150g cheese blend
+
1 oz | 28g fresh mozz

FOR EACH 12-INCH ROUND PIE WITH TOPPINGS:

⅔ cup | 150g sauce
+
¾ cup | 80g cheese blend

FOR EACH GRANDMA PIE WITH TOPPINGS:

⅔ cup | 150g sauce
+
3 oz | 84g fresh mozz

FOR EACH SICILIAN PIE WITH TOPPINGS:

⅔ cup | 150g sauce
+
Scant 1¼ cups | 125g cheese blend
+
1 oz | 28g fresh mozz

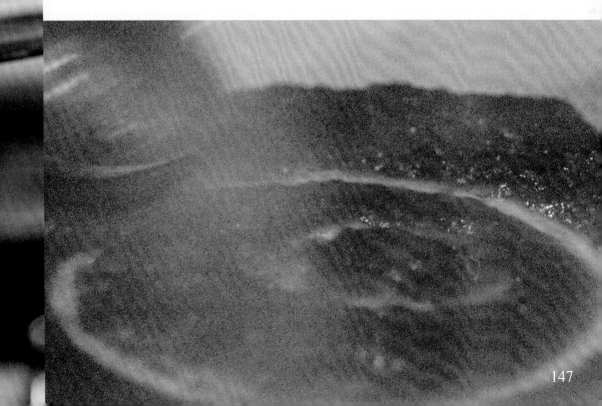

EXTRAS

I like to minimize food waste as much as possible and try to use up everything at the shop when I can. We always have a lot of dough on hand. I recommend repurposing it into sides and apps. You can make Vegan Garlic Knots (page 156), just like we do in the shop, and Focaccia (page 158), which is one of my favorite ways to use up dough at home.

Or you can change up Focaccia one more time into breadsticks or croutons to go with Tomato Soup (page 173), which uses elements from both Pizza Sauce (page 94) and Vegan Vodka Sauce (page 96).

The toppings can also be reused in a lot of ways. Think of them as not just prep for pizza but also as shortcuts to other meals. This chapter includes recipes for Chicken Parm (page 165), Eggplant Parm (page 166), and Meatball Parm (page 162), with options for serving them as sides or as heroes, all starting with recipes from the Toppings chapter. The Psyche Summer Salad (page 170) uses store-bought pizza toppings you might already have on hand.

You can feed yourself for a long time, really well, for cheap by using what you have.

CALZONE

A calzone is basically a folded-over pizza. When you've become an expert at making rounds and squares, try this. Calzones are also a great way to save pizza dough that you've accidentally torn and can't fix, or the dough stretched out into a weird shape. Just fold it over and turn it into a calzone.

Even though you're only putting the toppings on half of the dough, you can actually use the equivalent amount of cheese—if not more—that you would use on a pizza of the same size. So for a 12-inch calzone, which uses the same size dough ball as a 12-inch round pie, you can plan for at least a 1 cup | 100g shredded cheese.

The secret to a great calzone is what you put in it. Avoid anything that's runny or has a high water content. So, no raw veggies. But you can partially cook vegetables 50 to 70 percent and then use them as part of the filling.

I like to keep my calzone filling to mostly cheese, like a mix of our Cheese Blend (page 107) and fresh mozz or our Ricotta (page 104). Make sure your fresh mozz is sliced and has dried out a little. You shouldn't be pulling it out of a container of brine right before you put it into the calzone. Roasted Red Peppers (page 110) are delicious too, and broccoli rabe and Italian Chicken Sausage (page 119) is a classic combo.

Any kind of charcuterie just gets hot and sweaty in there, so I don't like to use pepperoni because it never cooks.

Sauce doesn't go in a calzone, but make sure you serve a generous amount of sauce on the side for dipping. Try it with our Pizza Sauce (page 94) or Vegan Vodka Sauce (page 96).

TIMING

About 15 to 20 minutes from the first stage (opening) to the final stage (cooking).

To start, you'll need one dough ball rested for at least 12 hours in the fridge—ideally 24 to 48 hours—and then brought to room temperature.

One hour before you plan to bake, preheat the oven to 550°F with the pizza steel in it on the middle rack. (Some home ovens won't get to 550°F, so preheat to how high your oven will go.) Slide a rack into the top position too, for broiling.

If you don't have a pizza steel, you can use a pizza stone, sheet pan, or a cast-iron pan turned upside down (see full details in Tools on page 46).

MAKES

One 12-inch-long calzone

EQUIPMENT

Pizza steel
Wooden pizza peel
Metal pizza turning peel

INGREDIENTS

1 dough ball from Dough recipe (page 61)

Scant 1 cup | 100g Cheese Blend (page 107), Ricotta (page 104), fresh mozz or a mix of cheeses

Fillings of your choice, in similar amounts as for pizza, for example, ½ cup Italian Chicken Sausage (page 119), ¼ cup Roasted Red Peppers (page 110) or Cremini Mushrooms (page 108)

Sauce for serving

1. Following the instructions in the Dough chapter, open up the dough and stretch it into a 12-inch round pie (see page 70). Transfer the dough to a wooden pizza peel.

2. Pile up the cheese on half of the round dough. Make sure to leave about 1½ inches uncovered along the edge. This is where you're going to fold and seal the calzone.

3. Add any additional fillings on top of the cheese. Aim to pile high rather than spread across to make sure you have enough dough on the edge to seal the whole thing.

4. Now fold the uncovered half of the dough over the cheese and fillings. Using your thumb and index finger, pinch and squeeze all the way along the rim to close the calzone. You can also use the end of a wooden stick or a fork to crimp the edges closed. You want to make sure nothing leaks out.

5. Using a fork, and working evenly across the calzone, poke the top a few times so steam can escape during baking.

6. Just like you would a regular pizza, wiggle the calzone on the pizza peel to make sure it can launch properly.

7. Following the instructions and guidance in the Baking Rounds section of Dough (page 72), bake for 7 to 8 minutes, until golden brown. And just like you would a regular pizza, make sure to check the bottom of the calzone as it browns. Use the metal turning peel to check the bottom and also to rotate the calzone during the cooking time so it bakes evenly. Move it to the top rack after the bottom firms up to finish the bake.

8. Pull the calzone from the oven and land it on a wooden cutting board or similar work surface. Slice and serve immediately with the sauce for dipping.

STORAGE

Just like pizza, a calzone is best eaten fresh. But if you have leftover calzone, let cool, wrap tightly in plastic wrap, and freeze for up to 2 months. Don't put it in the fridge. It keeps best when frozen fresh.

REHEATING

Follow the skillet method (see page 146) and reheat on the stove top. Or reheat in the oven or toaster oven. You can flip the calzone over halfway through the reheating process if you want to toast both sides.

VEGAN GARLIC KNOTS

One of my pizza guys came up with the idea to make our garlic knots vegan. With most pizza shops, people put pec or parm in theirs. As long as the dough is really good, people don't realize the cheese is missing. The freshly ground black pepper gives it a nice bite too.

MAKES
7 to 8 garlic knots

EQUIPMENT
Quarter or half sheet pan
Rolling pin (optional)
Pizza cutter or knife

INGREDIENTS
¼ cup | 52g olive oil, plus more for oiling the pan and work surface
1 dough ball from Dough recipe (page 61)
10 to 12 cloves garlic, separated, peeled, and minced
¼ cup | 15g minced fresh flat-leaf parsley
Kosher salt and black pepper
Pizza Sauce (page 94) for serving (optional)

1. Lightly oil a quarter sheet pan and your work surface.

2. Take out your dough ball and flatten it to about ½-inch thickness on your work surface. You can use your fingers or, for more consistency, a rolling pin.

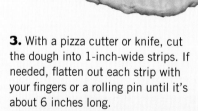

3. With a pizza cutter or knife, cut the dough into 1-inch-wide strips. If needed, flatten out each strip with your fingers or a rolling pin until it's about 6 inches long.

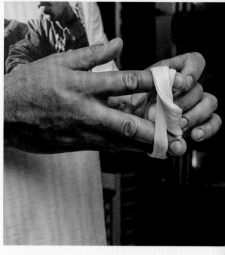

4. Working with one strip at a time, place two fingers of one hand in the center of the strip and, using your other hand, make an X across your two fingers by draping the ends of the strip across each other. Tuck one end into the loop you've created to tie your knot, then carefully slip your fingers out and tighten the knot. Finally, tuck the ends of the strip underneath the knot.

5. Place the knots on the prepared sheet pan, spacing them evenly 1 to 2 inches apart. Loosely wrap the knots on the sheet pan in plastic wrap. Let it proof in a warm spot for 2 to 3 hours. The knots should about double in size, appearing full and puffy.

6. While the dough is proofing, make the garlic-parsley oil. In a large bowl—you'll want something big enough to hold all the knots—combine the oil, garlic, and parsley. Set aside.

7. Preheat the oven to 425°F with a rack in the middle position.

8. When the knots have proofed and expanded in size, unwrap the pan. If the dough has stuck to the plastic wrap during this proof, gently peel it away so the dough doesn't shrink back. Bake the knots for about 10 minutes, until golden brown, rotating the pan from front to back halfway through the bake.

9. Remove the knots from the oven and immediately add them to the

bowl of parsley-garlic oil. Toss until evenly coated, adding salt and pepper to taste.

10. Serve the garlic knots immediately. You can also add a side of pizza sauce for dipping if you like.

At the shop, we also serve garlic knots with fresh mozz melted on top. Just drape a few slices of fresh mozz over the top of the knots at the end of baking and broil for 1 to 2 minutes. It's not vegan friendly, but it's delicious.

STORAGE

Store in airtight containers or plastic zip bags with all the air squeezed out in the freezer for up to 2 months.

REHEATING

Reheat the garlic knots on an oiled sheet pan in the oven or toaster oven at 350°F for 8 to 10 minutes, or until soft and warmed through. Toss again with more olive oil and pepper to taste, then serve immediately.

FOCACCIA

Focaccia is a great way to get more use out of your dough, and it's a simple bread to make if you're getting into other at-home baking besides pizza. You can use it for sandwiches, and it's great eaten on its own.

Time will do most of the work for you in this recipe. Keep in mind that you'll need to start the process the night before you want to bake.

I recommend starting with one 475g dough ball from the Sicilian recipe for this, which will give you a tall, fluffy focaccia when it's stretched and baked in a quarter sheet pan. The first few steps for stretching the dough in the pan aren't that different from prepping for Sicilians, actually.

You can also make a very crunchy, flatter version using one 360g dough ball from the Dough recipe (page 61). After you've baked it, cut it into strips or roughly tear into 1- or 2-inch pieces (see note at the end of this recipe) and serve it on top of or alongside Tomato Soup (page 173) or the Psyche Summer Salad (page 170).

TIMING
You'll be stretching, oiling, and salting for only 10 minutes across the whole process, but you'll need to plan for the overnight proof time plus an hour or two the next morning for a final proof.

To start, you'll need one dough ball rested for at least 12 hours in the fridge—ideally 24 to 48 hours—and then brought to room temperature.

A pizza steel isn't required for this recipe, but if you are using one, make sure to preheat the oven for 1 hour before you plan to bake.

MAKES
One 13-by-9-inch sheet

EQUIPMENT
Quarter sheet pan or similar-size baking dish (13 by 9 inches)

INGREDIENTS
1 dough ball from Sicilian dough recipe (page 80)
4 tbsp | 52g olive oil for the dough, or more as needed, plus more for oiling the pan and to finish (optional)
Flaky sea salt for topping

The night before you bake

1. Lightly oil a quarter sheet pan.

2. Place the dough ball in the pan and gently flatten it with your palm, pressing down once or twice. Similar to baking square pies, you're just pushing the dough down to help get out any air bubbles and to get it ready for the next step.

3. Drizzle about 1 tbsp | 13g of the oil over the dough, coating it lightly and evenly.

4. Loosely wrap the pan with the flattened dough ball in plastic wrap. Try to keep the plastic wrap from touching the dough. Let the dough rest at room temperature for 1 hour so it can relax.

5. When the dough is ready, remove the plastic wrap. Using all your fingertips, and working your way up and down lengthwise, lightly push down and outward on the dough until it is stretched the length of the pan.

6. Continue to push down on the dough until it evenly fills the entire pan.

7. Lightly drizzle the dough with about 1 tbsp | 13g of the oil.

8. Loosely cover the dough in its pan with plastic wrap and let rest at room temperature for 8 to 12 hours.

When you're ready to bake

1. Preheat the oven to 500°F with a rack in the middle position.

2. Check on your dough. It should have doubled in size. If it hasn't, let it keep proofing near the oven as the oven preheats, checking on it every 20 to 30 minutes to see how it's rising.

3. When the dough is about double in size—it should rise to the rim of the sheet pan—it's ready for the final step. Remove the plastic wrap.

4. For the final step, you're going to dot your fingertips all over the dough. This is how you get the craggy parts and pools of oil that make focaccia tasty. Working from one end of the pan to the other, use your fingertips to dimple the dough. Push all the way down to the bottom of the pan. Repeat so the dough is evenly covered in dimples about ½ inch apart.

5. Drizzle the remaining 2 tbsp | 26g oil evenly over the dough, filling the dimples you've just made.

6. Generously sprinkle the salt all over the dough (about 1 tsp).

7. Slide the pan into the oven and bake for 12 to 15 minutes, until golden brown, rotating the pan from front to back halfway through the bake.

8. Pull the focaccia from the oven and let cool for 2 to 3 minutes. Drizzle with more oil if you like.

9. Cut into squares and serve on their own, or split horizontally to make sandwiches.

STORAGE
Focaccia tastes best the day it is made, but you can store it in a paper bag on the counter.

Slice day-old focaccia into strips for breadsticks or roughly tear it into chunks for croutons. With either, drizzle the stale bread with olive oil and then toast in a dry skillet over medium heat until fragrant and golden brown.

WHAT TO DO IF THE DOUGH IS TOUCHING THE PLASTIC

The dough may have risen to the point that it's touching the plastic wrap. If it is, make sure to gently and slowly peel back the plastic. If you do it too quickly, the dough might get shocked and shrink back or deflate. If it does shrink back or deflate, it's not the end of the world. Carefully adjust the dough if you need to, making sure it fills the pan corner to corner, then let it rise again uncovered. Check on it every 20 to 30 minutes to see how it's rising.

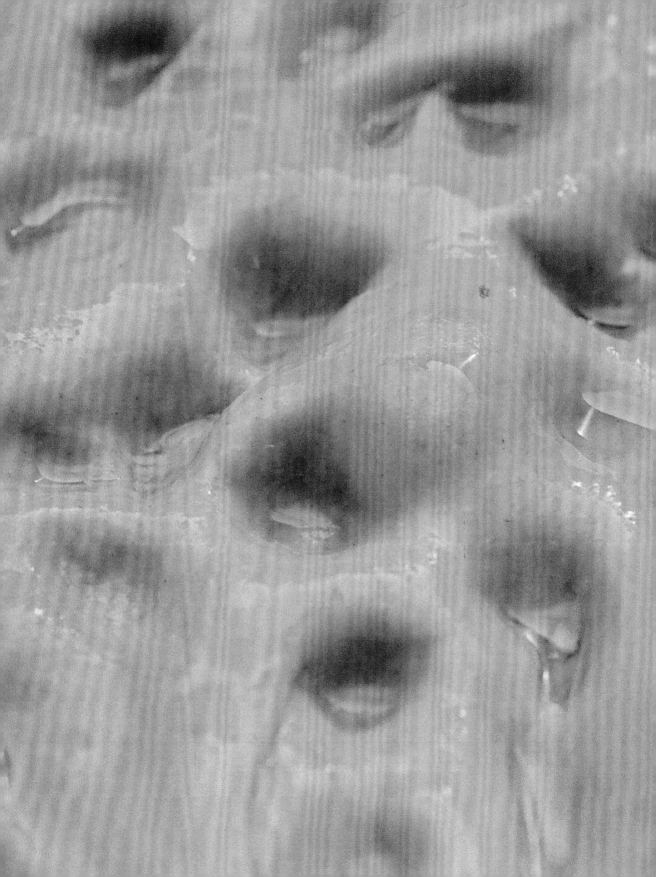

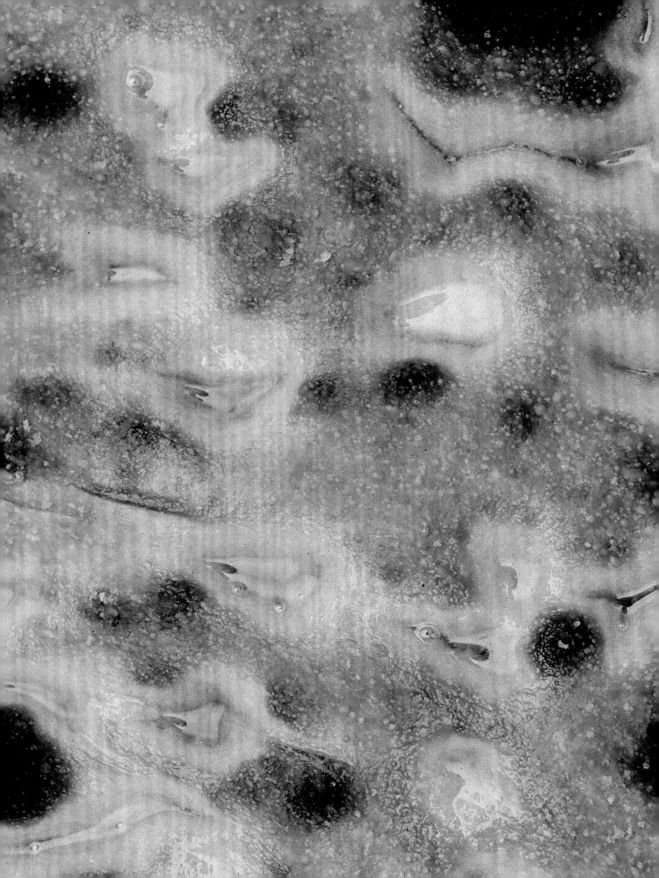

MEATBALL PARM SIDE OR HERO

This is another classic that I think should be on every slice shop's menu. Since you're using Meatballs (page 116) that have already been simmered in Pizza Sauce (page 94), I recommend topping them off with a little less sauce than the Chicken Parm (page 165) or Eggplant Parm (page 166). But you can hit them with more of the fresh sauce when they come out of the oven during the finishing to build layers of tomato flavor at varying stages.

TIMING
About 15 minutes.

A pizza steel is not required for this recipe, but if your steel lives in the oven, make sure to preheat the oven for a full hour.

For a side

1. Preheat the oven to 450°F.

2. Place the cooked meatballs in a medium cast-iron skillet or quarter sheet pan. Top the meatballs with the extra sauce, then sprinkle with the pec. Arrange the mozz evenly across the meatballs.

3. Bake for 6 to 8 minutes, until the meatballs are warmed through and the cheese is melted and bubbling.

4. Remove from the oven. Transfer the meatball parm to a plate or shallow bowl. Top them off with a spoonful of fresh sauce for contrast if you like, then finish with a drizzle of oil, more pec, and the basil. Serve immediately.

For a hero

1. Following the instructions for the meatball parm side, top the meatballs with the sauce, the pec, and the mozz and bake for 6 to 8 minutes.

2. While the meatball parm is baking, split the hero roll horizontally and scoop out the majority of the interior crumb. This gives you more room for the meatball parm (and you're not filling up on bread). If you're using focaccia, use a square large enough to hold the meatball parm and split it horizontally.

3. Take the roll or focaccia and drizzle the oil over the cut sides of the bread, then toast until golden brown. You can toast the bread alongside the meatballs in the same pan if there's room. You can also toast it directly on the oven rack. Keep an eye on it so it doesn't burn. Pull it out when it's ready, usually after a few minutes, and let the meatball parm keep cooking.

4. To assemble the sandwich, arrange the meatballs with their sauce and melted cheese on top of the bottom half of the toasted bread. Top them off with a spoonful of fresh sauce for contrast if you like, then finish with a drizzle of oil, more pec, and the basil. Close with the top half of the bread.

5. Cut the hero in half and transfer to a plate. Serve immediately.

MAKES
One side of meatball parm or one hero

EQUIPMENT
Medium cast-iron skillet or quarter sheet pan

INGREDIENTS
3 Meatballs (page 116), fully cooked in sauce
⅓ cup | 50g Pizza Sauce (page 94), or more as desired
2 to 3 tsp | 3 to 5g grated pec or parm, plus more to finish
4 to 6 slices fresh mozz, ⅛ to ¼ inch thick
Fresh basil to finish
Olive oil to finish and for the bread if using
1 hero roll or Focaccia square (page 158), if making a sandwich

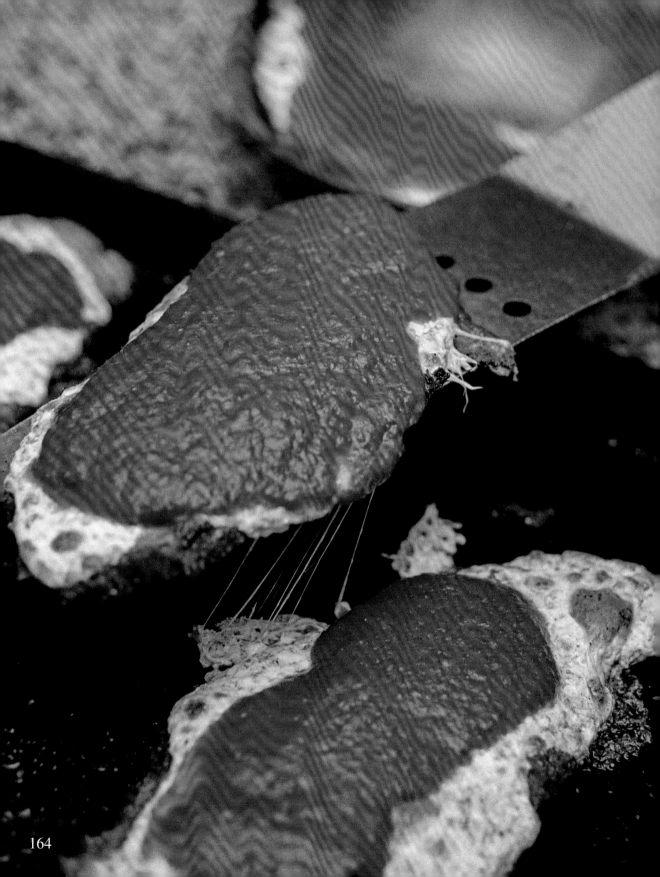

CHICKEN PARM SIDE OR HERO

Everyone should have a go-to chicken parm recipe. This one's ours. It's the perfect combination of salty, crunchy, and cheesy. It has the classic flavors of any old-school shop's chicken parm but with better ingredients.

You can also make a less traditional version by serving it on Focaccia (page 158) instead of a hero roll. Or you can serve the chicken parm as a side, with just sauce and cheese. It's delicious any of these ways.

For a side

1. Preheat the oven to 450°F. Lightly oil a medium cast-iron skillet or quarter sheet pan.

2. Place the breaded chicken cutlets in the prepared pan. Top the cutlets with the sauce, then sprinkle with the pec. Arrange the mozz evenly across the cutlets.

3. Bake for 6 to 8 minutes, until the chicken is warmed through and the cheese is melted and bubbling.

4. Remove from the oven. Transfer the chicken parm to a plate or shallow bowl. Top them off with a spoonful of fresh sauce for contrast if you like, then finish with a drizzle of oil, more pec, and the basil. Serve immediately.

For a hero

1. Following the instructions for the chicken parm side, top the cutlets with the sauce, the pec, and the mozz and bake for 6 to 8 minutes.

2. While the chicken parm is baking, split the hero roll horizontally and scoop out the majority of the interior crumb. This gives you more room for the chicken parm (and you're not filling up on bread). If you're using focaccia, use a square large enough to hold the chicken parm and split it horizontally.

3. Take the roll or focaccia and drizzle oil over the cut sides of the bread, then toast it until golden brown. You can toast the bread alongside the chicken in the same pan if there's room. You can also toast it directly on the oven rack. Keep an eye on it so it doesn't burn. Pull it out when it's ready, usually after a few minutes, and let the chicken parm keep cooking.

4. To assemble the sandwich, arrange the chicken with the sauce and melted cheese on top of the bottom half of the toasted bread. Top them off with a spoonful of fresh sauce for contrast if you like, then finish with a drizzle of oil, more pec, and the basil. Close with the top half of the bread.

5. Cut the hero in half and transfer to a plate. Serve immediately.

TIMING

About 15 minutes.

A pizza steel is not required for this recipe, but if your steel lives in the oven, make sure to preheat the oven for a full hour.

MAKES

One side of chicken parm or one chicken parm hero

EQUIPMENT

Medium cast-iron skillet or quarter sheet pan

INGREDIENTS

Olive oil for oiling the pan, for the bread if using, and to finish

2 to 3 cutlets Breaded Chicken (page 113)

⅔ cup | 150g Pizza Sauce (page 94), or more as desired

2 to 3 tsp | 3 to 5g grated pec or parm, plus more to finish

4 to 6 slices fresh mozz, ⅛ to ¼ inch thick

Fresh basil leaves to finish

1 hero roll or Focaccia square (page 158), if making a sandwich

EGGPLANT PARM SIDE OR HERO

Eggplant parm is delicious on its own. The crunch of the eggplant combined with the saltiness of the pec and fresh mozz, with the tomato sauce cutting through it and the freshness of the basil—it's classic.

Our Fried Eggplant (page 114) starts with slices of Italian- or American-style eggplant. They're thin but big—about the size of the bottom of a coffee cup or the palm of your hand. If you're using a smaller, skinnier eggplant variety, you can double up the number of slices for each side or sandwich.

For a side

1. Preheat the oven to 450°F. Lightly oil a medium cast-iron skillet or quarter sheet pan.

2. Place the fried eggplant slices in the pan. Top the eggplant with the sauce, then sprinkle with the pec. Arrange the mozz evenly across the eggplant slices.

3. Bake for 6 to 8 minutes, until the eggplant is warmed through and the cheese is melted and bubbling.

4. Remove from the oven. Transfer the eggplant parm to a plate or shallow bowl. Top them off with a spoonful of fresh sauce for contrast if you like, then finish with a drizzle of oil, more pec, and the basil. Serve immediately.

For a hero

1. Following the instructions for the eggplant parm side, top the fried eggplant with the sauce, the pec, and the mozz and bake for 6 to 8 minutes.

2. While the eggplant parm is baking, split the hero roll horizontally and scoop out the majority of the interior crumb. This allows more room for the eggplant parm (and you're not filling up on bread). If using focaccia, use a square large enough to hold the eggplant and split it horizontally.

3. Take the roll or focaccia and drizzle oil over the cut sides of the bread, then toast until golden brown. You can toast the bread alongside the fried eggplant in the same pan if there's room. You can also toast it directly on the oven rack. Keep an eye on it so it doesn't burn. Pull it out when it's ready, usually after a few minutes, and let the eggplant parm keep cooking.

4. To assemble the sandwich, arrange the eggplant with the sauce and melted cheese on top of the bottom half of the toasted bread. Top them off with a spoonful of fresh sauce for contrast if you like, then finish with a drizzle of oil, more pec, and the basil. Close with the top half of the bread.

5. Cut the hero in half and transfer to a plate. Serve immediately.

TIMING
About 15 minutes.

A pizza steel is not required for this recipe, but if your steel lives in the oven, make sure to preheat the oven for a full hour.

MAKES
One side of eggplant parm or one eggplant parm hero

EQUIPMENT
Medium cast-iron skillet or quarter sheet pan

INGREDIENTS
Olive oil for oiling the pan, for the bread if using, and to finish

4 to 5 slices Fried Eggplant (page 114)

⅔ cup | 150g Pizza Sauce (page 94), or more as desired

2 to 3 tsp | 3 to 5g grated pec or parm, plus more to finish

4 to 6 slices fresh mozz, ⅛ to ¼ inch thick

Fresh basil leaves to finish

Olive oil to finish

1 hero roll or Focaccia square (page 158), if making a sandwich

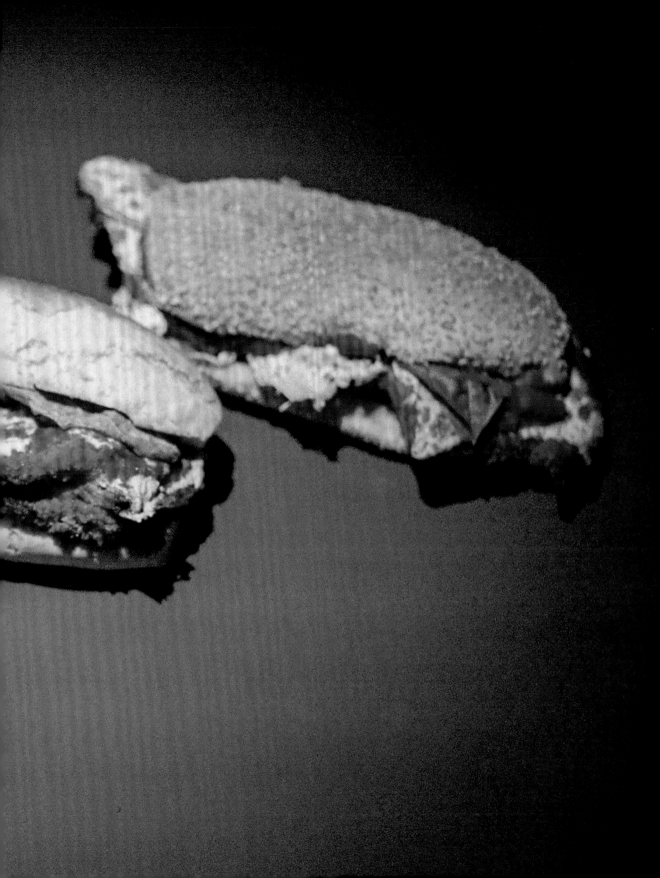

PSYCHE SUMMER SALAD

If you have access to heirloom tomatoes, good cheese, and an olive oil you really love, make this salad. If you're in New York and it's any other time of the year beyond that tiny window where heirloom tomatoes are in season, don't do it.

I mean you can, but this is all about peak tomato season and good olive oil. A winter tomato or a hothouse tomato, even if it's heirloom or organic, just won't be the same.

This salad was inspired by my friend Theo, one of the founders of Psyche Organic olive oil. It's not peppery, and it's round, fruity, and balanced, which I prefer. His family in Greece have been growing olives for years.

This salad is a play on a classic Italian tomato-mozz and a Greek salad combo. Besides the feta and kalamata olives, these are all ingredients we have on hand at the shop, so it's a smart way to repurpose toppings. It's also a great side or appetizer if you want something refreshing with pizza.

The seasoning for this recipe is more or less to taste, and you build the salad in the bowl you plan to serve it in.

TIMING
About 10 minutes.

We make this at the shop with ingredients we have on hand. Set aside a couple of extra minutes if you need to slice the red onion.

MAKES
One salad that's a generous light lunch for one person or enough for two or three people to share as a side

INGREDIENTS
1 large, in-season heirloom tomato
4 oz | 114g fresh mozz (½ medium-size ball)
8 or 9 pitted whole Kalamata olives
1 to 2 tbsp | 3 to 6g slivered red onion (thinly sliced, then cut into 1- to 2-inch lengths)
Pinch of kosher salt
Pinch of black pepper
Pinch of dried oregano
High-quality olive oil to finish
Red wine vinegar to finish
4 to 5 fresh basil leaves
3½ oz | 100g Greek feta cheese (half of a 7 oz | 200g package)

1. Cut the heirloom tomato into quarters, removing the stem and any hard core parts. Slice the quarters in half again to create eighths and place in a small serving bowl.

2. Cut the mozz into approximately 1-inch cubes and add to the bowl, scattering them on top and among the tomato chunks.

3. Slice the olives in half and sprinkle them over the tomato and mozz. Then sprinkle the red onion on top. Season with the salt, pepper, and oregano, adjusting the amounts to taste.

4. Drizzle everything with the oil followed by the vinegar, adding them to taste. Be generous with the oil. It's the star here.

5. Tear the basil leaves and scatter them on top. Cut the feta into rectangles or desired size and add evenly on top of the salad. Serve immediately.

TOMATO SOUP

Back in the day when I was working in other shops, I used to take leftover tomato sauce and make this soup at home. I added heavy cream back then, but this is an updated version using ingredients already on hand that are vegan. This recipe uses the thick cashew cream that goes into the Vegan Vodka Sauce (page 96), thinned out with water—basically, deconstructed cashew milk.

This soup goes well with a side of Focaccia (page 158). If you've got all these things at home, you've got lunch.

I prefer this soup when the tomato really comes through, with just a touch of cream. You can always add more cashew cream if you want a creamier soup.

1. In a small saucepan over medium-high heat, bring the Pizza Sauce to a simmer. Cook for 3 to 4 minutes, stirring regularly. Add the cashew cream and continue to cook, stirring regularly, for 2 to 3 more minutes.

2. Because the tomato sauce and cashew cream are both thick, you can stir in a little water, 1 tbsp at a time, to thin out the soup until it's at your desired consistency. For different mouthfeel and flavor, you can also try using a nondairy milk instead of water.

3. Taste and add salt and pepper if needed. The sauce is already seasoned from when you first made it, so taste again after you've adjusted the proportions with the cashew cream and water.

4. Remove from the heat and ladle into bowls. Sprinkle with more pepper, then tear the basil leaves and scatter on top. Finish with a drizzle of oil if you like. Serve with squares of focaccia or croutons (see Storage, page 159) if desired.

STORAGE
Leftover soup will keep in an airtight container (preferably glass) for up to 3 to 5 days in the fridge.

REHEATING
To reheat, place over medium heat and warm gently, stirring often, until piping hot.

> ### *TIMING*
> About 15 minutes

MAKES
About 2 cups | 2 to 3 servings

INGREDIENTS
2 cups | 450g Pizza Sauce (page 94)

2 to 3 tbsp | 28 to 42g cashew cream (page 97), or more as desired

Water or coconut or other nondairy milk if needed

Kosher salt and black pepper (optional)

Fresh basil leaves to finish (optional)

Olive oil to finish

Focaccia (page 158), cut into squares or torn into croutons

THE NEIGHBORHOOD

I love seeing everyone hanging out at the shop and having a good time. It's not easy to make a spot that people want to be in, though. Some restaurants try to force it, especially if they have a lot of money to hire designers and buy the nicest furniture or whatever. But it's a combination of creating the space with the energy you want and having the right people run it.

Just like we didn't advertise that we mill our own flour, we've never had a sign or anything that said there was a bar in the back. I think we were the first New York slice shop to have a counter in the front and a bar in the back, and we were definitely the first slice shop to serve natural wine.

How the space looks and feels is a big part of it. With the original shop, we wanted everyone to be

comfortable. The design is a throwback to old-school pizzerias but not dated. We've got real wood paneling, classic red booths, a bar with swivel stools, and the lights are low but not too dim. People are always taking pictures of the space when they first walk in.

You've got to have good music too. It depends on who's working, but there's usually hip-hop and R & B. Maybe more high-energy, upbeat rap when the pizza guys are getting ready to open the shop, or new-school R & B when our managers are on. Plus old-school nineties when I'm there.

We like to keep it chill and low-key. The staff is attentive, but not fussy. People come by themselves and get a slice and a drink at the bar, or they get a booth with their friends and order a couple of pies and a bottle of wine. You can do your own thing here.

SCARR'S 2.0

I started thinking of a bigger space when we got more popular. I don't like seeing people wait too long, and we were getting lines down the block every day. I also wanted a spot that was more spacious. I'm 6'2" so when I go out to eat I don't like places where you're sitting on top of each other. Of course, I care if the food is good more than anything else. But if you're stacking tables and rushing people, I'll just take it to-go.

We signed the lease to the bigger space on Orchard Street in early 2020. At the time, I had no idea how I wanted to design it, but I knew I didn't want it to look the same as across the street. A lot of other spots started biting off of us. They were copying our style and colors. So I figured I'd switch it up.

I've been into style, art, and design from a young age. I picked up things while observing the environment around me. I learned all the fly guy stuff from my older cousins and read *The Source* and *i-D*. I still love that era and turn to those looks for inspiration. Nothing overstylized and everything simple enough that it looks timeless without being stiff.

I see what I like and I go for it, and I know how to put it all together. That thinking influences how I design my shops.

Right after signing the new lease, Meagan and I went to Tokyo for the first time. It was interesting to see how much appreciation the Japanese put into the quality of the food, how they design a space, and the attention to detail with everything.

We ended up at a ramen spot in Shibuya that had been open for decades. It was homey, with an old-school diner counter running through it and floor-to-ceiling enamel walls. That inspired how we designed our walls at the new space, but we broke it up with smoke mirrors. I picked off-white enamel so that the space wouldn't feel stark, and I added black trim. The color combo reminds me of my Aunt Sonia's Chanel collection. Vibing off the blue of the New York City colors, we mixed shades of cobalt throughout the space, like the dyed concrete floor, custom tabletops, and grout in the bathrooms.

When we were putting all the other pieces together and didn't have a bar yet, my friend Emmett, who was also in the process of designing his pizza spot, invited me out to a place in Philly that sold antique bars.

I was eying this blue, mirror-tiled bar with peach accents—but Emmett wanted it too. I wasn't going to try to influence him. But it all worked out. He ended up buying a vintage one from Brunswick, the company that used to make bowling lanes, and I got the one I liked. Now it's in our second shop. Once I installed it and I saw it in there, it just filled the void—perfect for the space, the flow, and the design.

Our lighting came together when we were visiting Meagan's parents in Colorado. I saw this 1970s or '80s chromatic chandelier on Denver's Antique Row. It made me think of getting dragged to clubs when I was a little kid by my dad, cousins, and uncles—not clubs exactly but restaurants that would turn into party spots at night. I bought that one and sent a photo to my friends Fabiana and Helena at Coming Soon, the design store around the corner from us, to see if they could help source more. Turns out a guy they work with had the exact ones in storage. They always know how to find me exactly what I want.

It's funny how things come together like that sometimes. I get inspiration from everywhere. I don't write anything down. Everything lives in my head, then when it's time to put it all together, it just clicks.

COCKTAILS

I always come back to this: keep it simple and do it really well. Just like our food, our drinks menu is pretty tight. We have beers, natural wines, and a few cocktails made fresh using the best ingredients.

Most people want something simple with their pizza anyways, so ours are nothing fancy. But they're good, strong, and go well with the food.

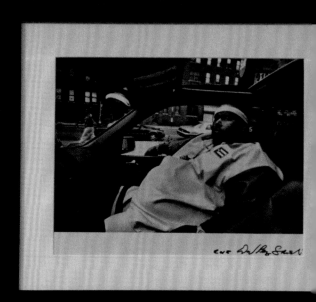

VEGAN PIÑA COLADA

Our colada is actually my mom's recipe that I made vegan. When we used to have family parties, this is one of the things everyone wanted her to make. It was what she was famous for.

She made it with dairy, but this version switches out the condensed milk in her recipe for coconut milk. She always used rum for a traditional piña colada. I used to drink Henny coladas growing up, but I swapped in D'Usse at the shop. You can use whichever Cognac you prefer.

You'll want freshly squeezed lime juice for this. One lime should yield about 1 ounce of juice. If your limes are small or dry, double up. If your lime feels hard or tight, try rolling it on the counter to help it release its juice before you cut it.

At the shop, we put the colada in a slushy machine, but I adapted it here to be easier to make at home and in two different ways. We've scaled it down so it can be poured over ice, or there's an option for making it frozen. Blending in the ice in the frozen version dilutes the original cocktail, so add more Cognac and/or vodka if you like it stronger. Or add more pineapple juice if you want something lighter.

Make sure all the ingredients are at room temperature. Coco López is sweetened cream of coconut and will separate when it's cold, so it's important that both the cream of coconut and the coconut milk are at room temperature for easier mixing.

TIMING
About 15 minutes

MAKES
6 servings over ice or
8 servings frozen

EQUIPMENT
Whisk
Upright blender (if making frozen)

INGREDIENTS
Ice cubes
7 oz Cognac of your choice
3 oz vodka of your choice
4 oz Coco López cream of
    coconut
13 oz pineapple juice
3½ oz unsweetened full-fat
    coconut milk
1½ oz fresh lime juice (about
    1 lime)

If serving over ice

1. Fill six 10-oz rocks glasses with ice all the way to the top.

2. In a pitcher, stir together the Cognac and vodka. Add the Coco López and whisk vigorously until thoroughly combined. The mixture will turn a cloudy, creamy light brown. You want to make sure these first three ingredients are mixed together really well. If they're not, they might separate later, and the fatty coconut will become clumps or chunks, which doesn't look that nice.

3. Add the pineapple juice and whisk again to combine. Add the coconut milk followed by the lime juice and then whisk one more time to combine.

4. Divide the colada mixture evenly among the ice-filled glasses and serve immediately.

If serving frozen

1. Place eight 12-oz tall glasses in the freezer to chill for 30 minutes.

2. Following the instructions for serving the coladas over ice, mix together all the liquid ingredients.

3. I recommend making these coladas in batches, depending on how much your blender can hold. In a blender, combine the colada mixture with ice. For each cocktail, use about 4 oz colada mixture and 1½ cups ice, for a slushy consistency. If you have crushed ice, use it instead of ice cubes. It'll be gentler on your blender. Taste and add more Cognac and/or vodka or pineapple juice to adjust the strength and consistency if needed.

4. Divide evenly among the chilled glasses and serve immediately.

STORAGE
For the nonfrozen colada version, you can keep the batched cocktail in an airtight container (preferably glass) for 1 to 2 days in the refrigerator. The mixture tends to separate, so when you're ready to serve it, whisk everything together again, then pour over ice if serving on the rocks or blend with ice for a frozen drink. The frozen colada is best served immediately.

ALCOHOL-FREE

Make the coladas alcohol-free by omitting the Cognac and vodka.

MAKES
4 servings over ice and 5 servings frozen

Ice cubes
4 oz Coco López
13 oz pineapple juice
3½ oz unsweetened full-fat coconut milk
1½ oz fresh lime juice (from about 1 lime)

If serving over ice, fill four 10-oz rocks glasses with ice all the way to the top. Following the instructions for alcohol-based coladas, whisk together the Coco López, pineapple juice, coconut milk, and lime juice, making sure to whisk the Coco López until it's smooth. Divide evenly among the ice-filled glasses and serve immediately.

If serving frozen, chill five 12-oz glasses in the freezer for 30 minutes. Whisk together all the liquid ingredients as directed for the alcohol-free version over ice, then blend as directed in the alcohol version, using about 4 oz colada mixture and 1½ cups ice for each cocktail. Divide evenly among the chilled glasses and serve immediately.

183

ALCOHOL-FREE

This lemonade that's equal parts fresh orange juice and lemon juice is great on its own.

MAKES
About 22 oz; 4 servings

Ice cubes
4 oz fresh lemon juice
4 oz fresh orange juice with the pulp strained out
4 oz simple syrup (see page 185)
10 oz cold water

Fill four 10-oz rocks glasses with ice all the way to the top.

In a pitcher, whisk together the lemon juice, orange juice, and simple syrup until thoroughly mixed. Whisk in the water, mixing well.

Divide evenly among the ice-filled glasses and serve immediately.

STORAGE
Store the batched cocktail in an airtight container (preferably glass) for 2 to 3 days in the refrigerator. When you're ready to serve it, whisk everything together again, then pour over ice.

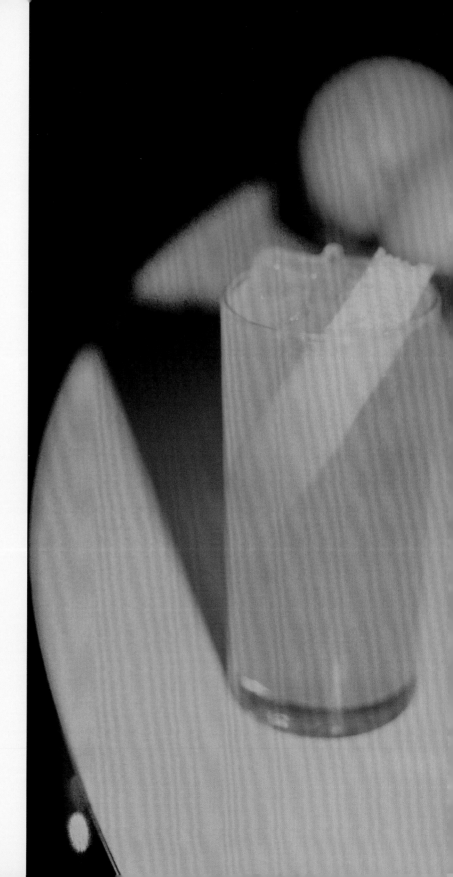

DJ CK LEMONADE

Clark was part of the inspiration for this recipe. A while ago he gifted me a bottle of D'Usse Cognac and told me how he and his wife always mix it with lemonade. Can't believe I never tried it before. It's an ode to them. We made a natural version with fresh-squeezed lemon and orange juice and unrefined sugar.

The lemonade goes down really easy, but it's strong. Make sure you serve it over lots of ice, which will dilute the drink as it melts.

You can keep the orange juice pulp if you want to, but I think it looks nicer strained out.

TIMING
About 15 minutes

MAKES
About 30 oz; six 5-oz servings

EQUIPMENT
Whisk

INGREDIENTS
Ice cubes
4 oz fresh lemon juice
4 oz fresh orange juice with the pulp strained out
4 oz simple syrup (recipe follows)
4 oz D'Usse or Cognac of your choice
4 oz vodka of your choice
10 oz cold water

1. Fill six 10-oz rocks glasses with ice all the way to the top.

2. In a pitcher, whisk the lemon juice, orange juice, and simple syrup together. Add the Cognac and vodka and whisk until thoroughly mixed. Finally, whisk in the water.

3. Divide evenly among the ice-filled glasses and serve immediately.

4. If you're serving the lemonade at a party in a pitcher, give it a stir before pouring.

SIMPLE SYRUP

Simple syrup is just one part water to one part sugar. To make simple syrup, combine 1 cup | 200g sugar and 1 cup | 237g water in a small sauce-pan, place over medium heat, and heat, stirring, until the sugar dissolves. Remove from the heat. You'll have about 1½ cups | 336g. Let it cool, then store in a tightly capped glass jar for up to 1 month in the refrigerator.

People usually use white granulated sugar, but I prefer coconut sugar or another less refined sugar. The ratio stays the same, but the color or flavor might be slightly different. If you're making simple syrup with an alternative sugar, taste it in this recipe and see how you like it.

GUAVA MARGARITA

This is the easiest cocktail recipe, and great for making a ton for a big party. Guava nectar is made from pureed guava pulp and you can usually find it at grocery stores in a can or carton. Depending on which brand you buy, it might be sweeter or thicker than what we use, so taste it and adjust the simple syrup or water as needed.

TIMING
About 15 minutes

MAKES
About 32 oz; six 5-oz servings

EQUIPMENT
Whisk

INGREDIENTS
Ice cubes
8½ oz tequila of your choice
2 oz triple sec
4 oz fresh lime juice
6 oz guava nectar
4 oz simple syrup (see page 185)
8 oz cold water
Pinch of salt

1. Fill six 10-oz rocks glasses with ice all the way to the top.

2. In a pitcher, whisk together the tequila, triple sec, lime juice, guava nectar, simple syrup, and water until thoroughly mixed.

3. Divide evenly among the ice-filled glasses and serve immediately.

STORAGE
Store the batched cocktail in an airtight container (preferably glass) for up to 2 to 3 days in the refrigerator. When you're ready to serve it, whisk everything together again, then pour over ice.

ALCOHOL-FREE

You can make this nonalcoholic by combining guava nectar and seltzer or sparkling water for more of a spritz. We do this at the shop for the kids who come in, and we serve it in the same glass as the regular margarita so they feel like they're having their own drink.

MAKES
About 5 oz; 1 serving

Ice cubes
3 oz guava nectar
2 oz bubbly water
1 lime

For each serving, fill a 10-oz rocks glass to the top with ice. Pour the guava nectar over the ice, top off with the bubbly water, or more as desired, stir, then finish with a squeeze of lime.

Thank you to my family, friends, and day ones who have supported me and the shop from the beginning. I wouldn't have any of this without you.

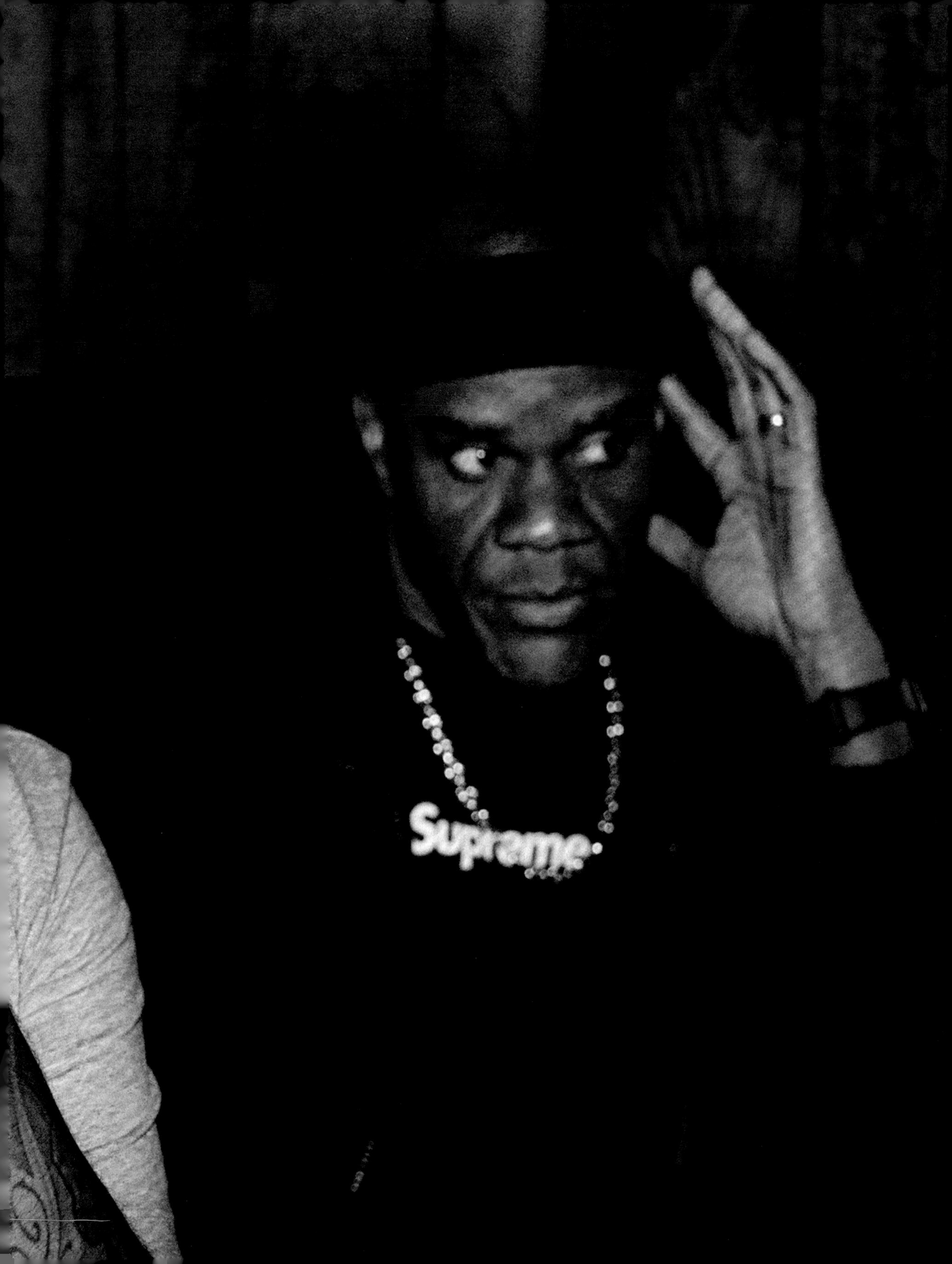
Supreme

ABOUT THE CONTRIBUTORS

ABOUT SCARR PIMENTEL

Born and raised in Manhattan, Scarr Pimentel grew up surrounded by family and friends in the food industry, which inspired his love for restaurants. After working in various spots Downtown, Scarr opened Scarr's Pizza on the Chinatown/LES border in 2016. With a focus on all-natural and organic ingredients, Scarr's Pizza is committed to creating high-quality products for the community and beyond.

ABOUT KIMBERLY CHOU TSUN AN

Kimberly Chou Tsun An is a writer, cultural worker, and community organizer. Steeped in Detroit and based in Brooklyn, she is a former journalist and a longtime codirector of Food Book Fair, a festival of writing about eating.

Kimberly is a founding member of FIG, a food justice collective that, among other things, facilitates political education for food workers and coordinates a free-food distribution program in partnership with folx in New York City and the Hudson Valley fighting for food sovereignty.

Her favorite slice is whatever just came out of the oven ripping hot—ideally, a square Hotboi, eaten outside with a cold seltzer after biking over the bridge. This is her first book.

ABOUT KOKI SATO

Koki Sato was born and raised in Tokyo, Japan. He graduated from the International Center of Photography in 2011 and began working as a fine artist and photographer based in New York, providing visuals for several brands and artists.

Koki published his first photo book, *99¢ City*, in 2016, and his second, *fragile*, in 2019. His most recent photo book, *NOSTALGIA*, which was published by Paradigm Publishing in 2021, was recognized with a book release event at Mast Books in New York and a solo exhibition at The Plug in Tokyo the same year. His most recent photo book, GYAKKO (逆光), was published by RISE ABOVE GALLERY in 2023. It also had a solo exhibition in Osaka and at AA in Tokyo the same year.

fresh hot pizza

fresh hot pizza

esh hot pizza

sh hot pizza

sh hot pizza

pizza

zza

INDEX

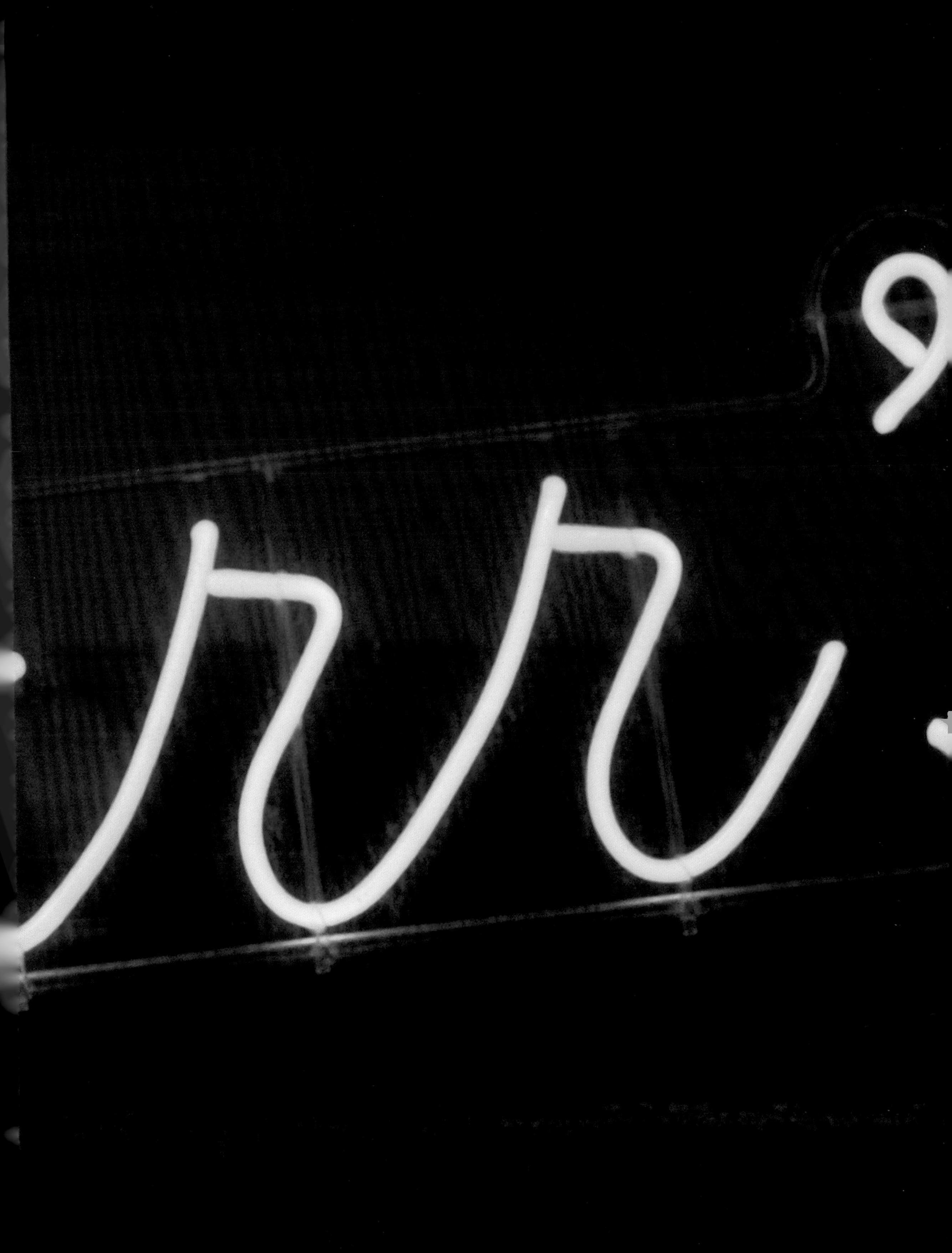

"*The Scarr's Pizza Cookbook* is a perfect peek inside the beautiful world of Scarr Pimentel. More than recipes, more than a story, this book is full of wonderful moments captured in time."

DANNY BOWIEN, chef

"I remember coming into the shop for the first time the first year it opened. Walked to the back, had a three-dollar cup of presidente and kinda never left. Scarr's Pizza slowly became a hub downtown, a place you can go where there will always be friends you can talk to and new people you can meet. For me it became a second home, and it's incredible to see how far it has come. The bones are new, but the soul and the homey feeling are still there. If you feel otherwise, you just don't know."

HUGO MENDOZA

"Scarr is a great human who has dedicated himself to the art of making perfect pizza. With *The Scarr's Pizza Cookbook*, he shares his elite New York–style knowledge and wisdom. He's a brother for life."

MATTY MATHESON, *New York Times* bestselling author of *Matty Matheson: A Cookbook* and *Matty Matheson: Home Style Cookery*

"A delicious dive into NYC life and culture. I'm talking about the Scarr's experience and his Sicilian slice recipe."

CAMILLE BECERRA, chef and pizzeria neighbor

"Scarr has worked his way from the back of New York's best pizza joints all the way to create his own legendary spot in LES. A man with this much taste? Come on, it's only right he drops a cookbook."

J.R. EWING, founder of Atlas Opera

"Like all great New York City tales, this book is a glimpse into the world of a quintessential neighborhood legend. Recipes to make damn fine pizza but, also, a blueprint on how to strive for impeccable taste, persevere, and succeed through an unwavering commitment to quality while being true to self. You want the best pizza in town? Go to Scarr's. You want to be amazed by one of the most genuine people and places in the game? Go to Scarr's."

GERARDO GONZALEZ, chef

"Scarr's is our oasis in the desert. It's the thing that saves us after forgetting to eat all day. When it's 4 p.m. and we're about to faint, there's our favorite slice that helps us get through the rest of the day. We can always count on Scarr's."

HELENA BARQUET & FABIANA FARIA, founders of Coming Soon